W9-AZP-610

*Everything you always
wanted to know about Heaven*

Everything you always
wanted to know about

HEAVEN

Randy Alcorn

Tyndale House Publishers, Inc.
Carol Stream, Illinois

Visit Tyndale online at www.tyndale.com.

TYNDALE, Tyndale's quill logo, and *LeatherLike* are registered trademarks of
Tyndale House Publishers, Inc.

Everything You Always Wanted to Know about Heaven

Copyright © 2008 by Eternal Perspective Ministries. All rights reserved.

Previously published in 2008 as *TouchPoints: Heaven* by Tyndale House
Publishers, Inc., under ISBN 978-1-4143-2360-2. First printing as
Everything You Always Wanted to Know about Heaven in 2014.

Cover photograph of clouds copyright © Ocean/Corbis. All rights reserved.

Designed by Mark Anthony Lane II

Unless otherwise indicated, Scripture quotations are taken from the *Holy Bible*,
New Living Translation, copyright © 1996, 2004, 2007, 2013 by Tyndale House
Foundation. Used by permission of Tyndale House Publishers, Inc., Carol Stream,
Illinois 60188. All rights reserved.

Scripture quotations marked NIV are taken from the Holy Bible, *New
International Version,*® NIV.® Copyright © 1973, 1978, 1984, 2011 by Biblica,
Inc.® Used by permission of Zondervan. All rights reserved worldwide.
www.zondervan.com.

Scripture quotations marked NKJV are taken from the New King James Version.®
Copyright © 1982 by Thomas Nelson, Inc. Used by permission. All rights reserved.

Scripture quotations marked ESV are taken from *The Holy Bible*, English
Standard Version® (ESV®), copyright © 2001 by Crossway, a publishing
ministry of Good News Publishers. Used by permission. All rights reserved.

Library of Congress Cataloging-in-Publication Data
Alcorn, Randy C.
  Everything you always wanted to know about heaven / Randy Alcorn.
    pages cm
  Includes index.
  ISBN 978-1-4143-9941-6 (sc)
  1. Heaven—Christianity—Miscellanea. I. Title.
  BT846.3.A425 2014
  236'.24—dc23   2014014368

Printed in China

20
9   8

Contents

Author's Note *xi*
Introduction *xiii*

PART I THE PRESENT HEAVEN
WHAT THE BIBLE SAYS ABOUT WHERE
WE GO FIRST WHEN WE DIE

What is the "present Heaven"? *3*

Are there actually two distinct Heavens? *5*

Do we remain conscious after death? *7*

Is the present Heaven a physical place? *10*

Do people have intermediate bodies in the intermediate
    Heaven? *14*

Will we be judged when we die? *19*

What is life like in the present Heaven? *22*

Do Heaven's inhabitants remember life on Earth? *24*

Do people in the present Heaven see what is happening
on Earth? 28

Do people in Heaven pray for those on Earth? 32

Can it be Heaven if people are aware of anything bad
on Earth? 33

Will we live in Heaven forever? 37

PART II THE ETERNAL HEAVEN
WHAT THE BIBLE SAYS ABOUT WHERE
WE WILL LIVE FOREVER

Where do we get our misconceptions about Heaven? 41

Is Heaven beyond our imagination? 43

If "no eye has seen" Heaven, how can we know about it? 45

Is the eternal Heaven an actual place? 48

Is Heaven our default destination . . . or is Hell? 50

Is Hell real? 52

What did Jesus say about Hell? 54

What will it mean to unite Heaven and Earth? 56

Will the old Earth be destroyed . . . or renewed? 58

Will the New Earth be familiar . . . like home? 62

What will it mean to see God in Heaven? 64

What will it mean for God to dwell among us? 68

Will God serve us? 71

How will we worship God in Heaven? 73

Will we actually rule with Christ in Heaven? *75*
How will we rule God's Kingdom? *78*

PART III LIFE ON THE NEW EARTH
A TOPICAL GUIDE TO OUR MANY QUESTIONS
ABOUT THE ETERNAL HEAVEN

Abilities *83*

Age *86*

Alien Life *88*

Angels *90*

Animals *92*

Anticipation *103*

Bodies *105*

Books and Reading *109*

Boredom *112*

Clothing *115*

Conflict *117*

Culture *119*

Desires *121*

Emotions *123*

Entertainment and Recreation *125*

Equality *128*

Family *130*

Food and Drink *132*

Free Will *135*

Friendships *137*

Gender *139*

Hell *141*

Homes *143*

Identity *145*

Knowledge and Learning *152*

Landmarks *157*

Languages *159*

Laughter and Fun *161*

Marriage *163*

Music *165*

Nature *168*

New Jerusalem *176*

Oceans *180*

Pets *183*

Physical Space *185*

Possessions *186*

Privacy *190*

Relationships *192*

Remembering the Old Earth *199*

Resurrection *204*

Rest *207*

Rewards *210*

Sex *212*

Sin 214

Sleep 216

Space and the Universe 218

Sports 225

Technology 227

Time 230

Time Travel 233

Tree of Life 235

Unfulfilled Dreams 238

Weather 240

Work 242

PART IV   CAN YOU KNOW YOU'RE GOING TO HEAVEN?

PART V   GOD'S PROMISES ABOUT HEAVEN

When you're wondering if there really is a Heaven . . . 259

When you're wondering what Heaven will be like . . . 260

When you're wondering if there's a place for you in
     Heaven . . . 261

When you're wondering if you will go to Heaven and how to
     get there . . . 262

When you're afraid of dying . . . 264

When you doubt there is life after death . . . 265

When you're searching for happiness that lasts . . . 266
When you long for something more than this world . . .267

Scripture Index 269
About the Author 275

Author's Note

THE MATERIAL IN this little book is just a slice of all you can discover from Scripture about what Heaven is like and what it will be like for God's people some day. With help from my editors, Jason and Ron Beers, what you see here is taken from my larger, more comprehensive book entitled *Heaven*. I hope that after you read *Everything You Always Wanted to Know about Heaven*, you'll be enriched and will be motivated to learn more and more about the amazing place our God of wonders is preparing for his children.

Introduction

IN THIS BOOK, we'll see from Scripture an exciting yet strangely neglected truth: God never gave up on his original plan for human beings to dwell on Earth. In fact, the climax of history will be the creation of new heavens and a New Earth—a resurrected universe inhabited by resurrected people living with the resurrected Jesus.

A pastor once confessed to me, "Whenever I think about Heaven, it makes me depressed. I'd rather just cease to exist when I die."

"Why?" I asked.

"I can't stand the thought of that endless tedium. To float around in the clouds with nothing to do but strum a harp . . . it's all so terribly boring. Heaven doesn't sound much better than Hell. I'd rather be annihilated than spend eternity in a place like that."

Where did this Bible-believing, seminary-educated pastor get such a view of Heaven? Certainly not from Scripture, where Paul said that to depart and be with Christ was far better than staying on a sin-cursed Earth (Philippians 1:23). My friend was more honest about it than most, yet I've found that many Christians share the same misconceptions about Heaven.

Jesus said of the devil, "When he lies, it is consistent with his character; for he is a liar and the father of lies" (John 8:44). Some of Satan's favorite lies are about Heaven. Satan need not convince us that Heaven doesn't exist. He need convince us only that Heaven is a place of boring, unearthly existence. If we believe that lie, we'll be robbed of our joy and anticipation, we'll set our minds on this life and not the next, and we won't be motivated to share our faith. Why should we share the "good news" that people can spend eternity in a boring, ghostly place even we're not looking forward to?

Fortunately, Jesus has come from Heaven to tell us about his Father, the world beyond, and the world to come. If we listen to him—which will require a concerted effort not to listen to the devil's lies—we will never be the same. Nor will we ever want to be. Satan cannot keep Christ from defeating him, but he can persuade us that Christ's victory is only partial, that God will abandon his original plan for mankind and Earth. Because Satan hates us, he's determined to rob us of the joy we'd have if we believed what God tells us about the magnificent world to come.

By the time you finish reading this book, you will have a biblical basis for envisioning the eternal Heaven. You will understand that in order to get a picture of Heaven—which will one day be centered on the New Earth—you don't need to look up at the clouds; you simply need to look around you and imagine what all this would be like without sin and death and suffering and corruption.

So look out a window. Take a walk. Use your God-given skills to paint or draw or build a shed or write a book. But imagine our world—all of it—in its original condition: The happy dog with the wagging tail, not the snarling beast, beaten and starved.

The flowers not wilted, the grass not dying, the blue sky without pollution. People smiling and joyful, not angry, depressed, and empty. If you're not in a particularly beautiful place, close your eyes and envision the most beautiful place you've ever been—complete with palm trees, raging rivers, jagged mountains, waterfalls, or snowdrifts.

Think of friends or family members who loved Jesus and are with him now. Picture them with you, walking together in this place. All of you have powerful bodies, stronger than those of Olympic decathletes. You are laughing, playing, talking, and reminiscing. You reach up to a tree to pick an apple or orange. You take a bite. It's so sweet that it's startling. You've never tasted anything so good. Now you see someone coming toward you. It's Jesus, with a big smile on his face. You fall to your knees in worship. He pulls you up and embraces you.

At last, you're with the person you were made for, in the place you were made to be. Everywhere you go, there will be new people and places to enjoy, new things to discover. What's that you smell? A feast. A party's ahead, and you're invited. There's exploration and work to be done—you can't wait to get started.

I have a biblical basis for all these statements, and for many more. After you examine what Scripture says, I hope that the next time you hear people say, "We can't begin to imagine what Heaven will be like," you'll be able to tell them, "I can."

PART I

The Present Heaven

WHAT THE BIBLE SAYS ABOUT WHERE
WE GO FIRST WHEN WE DIE

What is the "present Heaven"?

> *1 Thessalonians 4:13* . . . Dear brothers and sisters, we
> want you to know what will happen to the believers
> who have died so you will not grieve like people who
> have no hope.

> *Philippians 1:23* . . . I'm torn between two desires:
> I long to go and be with Christ, which would be far
> better for me.

The apostle Paul considered it vital for us to know what happens when we die: "Dear brothers and sisters, we want you to know what will happen to the believers who have died."

Most of this book will be centered on the eternal Heaven—the place where we will live forever after the final Resurrection. But because we've all had loved ones die, and we ourselves will die unless Christ returns first, we should consider what Scripture teaches about the present Heaven—the place Christians go when they die—and where they will live until the return of Christ and the final Resurrection.

When Christians die, they enter into what is often called the "intermediate state," a transitional period between their past lives on Earth and their future resurrection to life on the New Earth. By definition, an intermediate state or location is temporary. "Intermediate" does not mean a halfway place that's only sort of Heaven, but the place where we will live between our lives here and the "final" Heaven that will be centered on the New Earth.

Life in the Heaven we go to when we die is "far better" than living here on Earth under the Curse, away from the direct presence of God. Though it will be a wonderful place, the present Heaven is not the place we are made for, the place God promises to refashion for us to live in forever. God's children are destined for life as resurrected beings on a resurrected Earth.

Are there actually two distinct Heavens?

> *Revelation 21:1* . . . I saw a new heaven and
> a new earth, for the old heaven and the old
> earth had disappeared. And the sea was also
> gone.

Books on Heaven often fail to distinguish between the intermediate and the eternal states, using the one word—Heaven—as all-inclusive. But this keeps us from understanding important biblical distinctions.

In this book, when referring to the place believers go after death, I will sometimes use the theological phrase "intermediate Heaven," but more often I will say the "present Heaven." This is because the latter term seems less confusing to most people. However, both terms refer to exactly the same place.

The present Heaven is a temporary residence where departed saints live until the return of Christ and our bodily resurrection. The eternal Heaven, the New Earth, is our true home, the place where we will live forever with our Lord and one another. The great redemptive promises of God will find their ultimate fulfillment on the New Earth, not in the present Heaven.

Once we abandon our assumption that Heaven cannot change, it all makes sense. God does not change; he's immutable. But God clearly says that Heaven will change. It will eventually be relocated to the New Earth. Similarly, what we now refer to as Hell will also be relocated. After the Great White Throne Judgment, Hell will be cast into the eternal lake of fire (Revelation 20:14-15).

Do we remain conscious after death?

Ecclesiastes 12:7 . . . The dust will return to the earth, and the spirit will return to God who gave it.

Luke 16:22-24 . . . Finally, the poor man died and was carried by the angels to be with Abraham. The rich man also died and was buried, and his soul went to the place of the dead. There, in torment, he saw Abraham in the far distance with Lazarus at his side. The rich man shouted, "Father Abraham, have some pity! Send Lazarus over here to dip the tip of his finger in water and cool my tongue. I am in anguish in these flames."

Luke 23:43 . . . Jesus replied, "I assure you, today you will be with me in paradise."

2 Corinthians 5:8 . . . Yes, we are fully confident, and we would rather be away from these earthly bodies, for then we will be at home with the Lord.

At death, the human spirit goes either to Heaven or to Hell. Christ depicted Lazarus and the rich man as conscious in Heaven and in Hell immediately after they died. Jesus told the dying thief on the cross, "Today you will be with me in paradise." After their deaths, martyrs are pictured in Heaven, crying out to God to bring justice on Earth.

These passages make it clear that there is no such thing as "soul sleep," a long period of unconsciousness between life on Earth and life in Heaven. The phrase "falling asleep" has confused some. Given the passages that show ongoing consciousness after death, "falling asleep" is a euphemism for death, describing the body's outward appearance. The spirit's departure from the body ends our existence on Earth. The physical part of us "sleeps" until the final Resurrection, while the spiritual part of us relocates to a conscious existence in Heaven.

> *Revelation 6:9-10* . . . When the Lamb broke the fifth seal, I saw under the altar the souls of all who had been martyred for the word of God and for being faithful in their testimony. They shouted to the Lord and said, "O Sovereign Lord, holy and true, how long before you judge the people who belong to this world and avenge our blood for what they have done to us?"

Every reference in Revelation to human beings talking and worshiping in Heaven prior to the resurrection of the dead demonstrates that our spiritual beings are conscious, not sleeping, after death. Nearly everyone who believes in soul sleep believes that souls are disembodied at death. In the first place, it's not clear how disembodied beings could sleep because sleeping involves a physical body, and second, the mind continues to be active while asleep, as our dreams demonstrate.

Is the present Heaven a physical place?

Revelation 7:9 . . . I saw a vast crowd, too great to count, from every nation and tribe and people and language, standing in front of the throne and before the Lamb. They were clothed in white robes and held palm branches in their hands.

Revelation 8:6 . . . The seven angels with the seven trumpets prepared to blow their mighty blasts.

Revelation 8:13 . . . I looked, and I heard a single eagle crying loudly as it flew through the air.

Hebrews 8:5 . . . [Earthly priests] serve in a system of worship that is only a copy, a shadow of the real one in heaven. For when Moses was getting ready to build the Tabernacle, God gave him this warning: "Be sure that you make everything according to the pattern I have shown you here on the mountain."

If we look at Scripture, we'll see considerable evidence that the present Heaven has physical properties. We're told there are scrolls in Heaven, elders who have faces, martyrs who wear clothes, and even people with palm branches in their hands. There are musical instruments in the present Heaven, horses coming into and out of Heaven, and an eagle flying overhead in Heaven. Perhaps some of these objects are merely symbolic, with no corresponding physical reality. But is that true of all of them?

Many commentators dismiss the possibility that any of these passages in Revelation should be taken literally, on the grounds that the book of Revelation is apocalyptic literature, which is known for its figures of speech. But the book of Hebrews isn't apocalyptic, it's epistolary. Moses was told, in building the earthly Tabernacle, "Be sure that you make everything according to the pattern I have shown you here on the mountain." If that which was built after the pattern was physical, might it suggest the original was also physical? The book of Hebrews seems to say that we should see Earth as a derivative realm and Heaven as the source realm. If we do, we'll abandon the assumption that something existing in one realm cannot exist in the other. In fact, we'll consider it likely that what exists in one realm exists in at least some form in the other.

> *Hebrews 12:22* . . . You have come to Mount Zion, to the city of the living God, the heavenly Jerusalem, and to countless thousands of angels in a joyful gathering.

If we know that the New Jerusalem will be a physical city on the New Earth, and we also know that a city called Jerusalem is currently in the intermediate Heaven, doesn't that suggest this present city is physical?

> *Revelation 2:7* . . . To everyone who is victorious I will give fruit from the tree of life in the paradise of God.

The same physical tree of life that was in the Garden of Eden will one day be in the New Jerusalem on the New Earth (Revelation 22:2). Now, Revelation 2:7 tells us, the tree of life is (note the present tense) in the present Heaven. Shouldn't we assume the same tree, called by the same name, has the same physical properties it once had in the Garden of Eden and will have in the New Jerusalem? If it doesn't, could it really be called the tree of life?

Do people have intermediate bodies in the intermediate Heaven?

> *Genesis 2:7* . . . The LORD God formed the man from the dust of the ground. He breathed the breath of life into the man's nostrils, and the man became a living person.

Unlike God and the angels, who are in essence spirits (John 4:24; Hebrews 1:14), human beings are by nature both spiritual and physical. God did not create Adam as a spirit and place it inside a body. Rather, he first created a body, then breathed into it a spirit. There was never a moment when a human being existed without a body. We are not essentially spirits who inhabit bodies, we are essentially as much physical as we are spiritual. We cannot be fully human without both a spirit and a body.

Given the consistent physical descriptions of the intermediate Heaven and those who dwell there, it seems possible—though this is certainly debatable—that between our earthly lives and our bodily resurrection God may grant us some temporary physical form that will allow us to function as human beings while in that unnatural state "between bodies" awaiting our bodily resurrection. If so, that would account for the repeated depictions of people now in Heaven occupying physical space, wearing clothes and crowns, carrying branches, and having body parts (for example, Lazarus's finger in Luke 16:24).

> *Revelation 10:9-10* . . . I went to the angel and told him to give me the small scroll. "Yes, take it and eat it," he said. "It will be sweet as honey in your mouth, but it will turn sour in your stomach!" So I took the small scroll from the hand of the angel, and I ate it! It was sweet in my mouth, but when I swallowed it, it turned sour in my stomach.

It appears the apostle John had a body when he visited Heaven because he is said to have grasped, held, eaten, and tasted things there. To assume this is all figurative language is not a restriction demanded by the text but only a presupposition that Heaven isn't physical and people there don't have physical forms. This Revelation 10 account of John's eating a small scroll closely parallels Ezekiel 3:1-3. Of course, there is symbolic meaning to the eating of the scrolls by both Ezekiel and John, but the eating itself appears to have been literal.

> *2 Corinthians 12:3,* NIV ... Whether in the body or apart from the body I do not know, but God knows.

> *Acts 1:11* ... "Men of Galilee," they said, "why are you standing here staring into heaven? Jesus has been taken from you into heaven, but someday he will return from heaven in the same way you saw him go!"

A fundamental article of the Christian faith is that the resurrected Christ now dwells in Heaven. We are told that his resurrected body on Earth was physical and that this same, physical Jesus ascended to Heaven, from where he will one day return to Earth. It seems indisputable, then, to say that there is at least one physical body in the present Heaven. If Christ's body in the intermediate Heaven has physical properties, it stands to reason that others in Heaven could have physical forms as well, even if only temporary ones. If we know there is physical substance in Heaven (namely, Christ's body), can we not also assume that other references to physical objects in Heaven, including physical forms and clothing, are literal rather than figurative?

> *Hebrews 11:5* . . . It was by faith that Enoch was taken up to heaven without dying—"he disappeared, because God took him."

> *2 Kings 2:11-12* . . . As they were walking along and talking, suddenly a chariot of fire appeared, drawn by horses of fire. It drove between the two men, separating them, and Elijah was carried by a whirlwind into heaven. Elisha saw it . . . as they disappeared from sight.

Enoch and Elijah appear to have been taken to Heaven in their physical bodies. Apparently Enoch's body was not left behind to bury. The Septuagint translates it as Enoch "was not found." Similarly, Elijah was taken to Heaven without dying and without leaving a body behind. Given that at least one and perhaps three people now have bodies in Heaven, isn't it possible that others might be given physical forms as well?

To avoid any misunderstanding, I need to emphasize a critical doctrinal point. According to Scripture, we do *not* receive resurrection bodies immediately after death. Resurrection does not happen one at a time. *If* we have intermediate forms in the intermediate Heaven, they will not be our true bodies, which we leave behind at death. Continuity is only between our original and our resurrection bodies.

So *if* we are given material forms when we die (and I'm suggesting this possibility only because of the many Scriptures depicting physical forms in Heaven), they would be temporary vessels, perhaps comparable to the human-appearing bodies that angels sometimes take on. However, they would be distinct from our true bodies, which remain dead until the final Resurrection. Any understanding of people having physical forms immediately after death that would lead us to conclude that the future resurrection is unnecessary is emphatically wrong.

Will we be judged when we die?

> *Ephesians 2:8-9* . . . God saved you by his grace when you believed. And you can't take credit for this; it is a gift from God. Salvation is not a reward for the good things we have done, so none of us can boast about it.

> *Titus 3:5* . . . He saved us, not because of the righteous things we had done, but because of his mercy. He washed away our sins, giving us a new birth and new life through the Holy Spirit.

When we die, we face judgment, sometimes called the judgment of faith. The outcome of this judgment determines whether we go to the present Heaven or the present Hell. This initial judgment depends not on our works but on our faith, which itself is called a gift of God. It is not about what we've done during our lives but about what Christ has done for us. If we have accepted Christ's atoning death for us, then when God judges us after we die, he sees his Son's sacrifice for us, not our sin. Salvation is a free gift, to which we can contribute absolutely nothing. We have only to humbly receive the gift.

Romans 14:10-12 . . . Why do you condemn another
believer? Why do you look down on another believer?
Remember, we will all stand before the judgment seat
of God. For the Scriptures say, "'As surely as I live,'
says the LORD, 'every knee will bend to me, and every
tongue will declare allegiance to God.'" Yes, each of
us will give a personal account to God.

2 Corinthians 5:10 . . . We must all stand before
Christ to be judged. We will each receive whatever
we deserve for the good or evil we have done in this
earthly body.

1 Corinthians 3:13-14 . . . On the judgment day, fire
will reveal what kind of work each builder has done.
The fire will show if a person's work has any value. If
the work survives, that builder will receive a reward.

The first judgment, of faith, is not to be confused with
the final judgment, sometimes called the judgment
of works. Both believers and unbelievers face a final
judgment. The Bible indicates that all believers will
stand before the judgment seat of Christ to give an

account of their lives. It's critical to understand that this judgment is a judgment of works, not of faith. Our works do not affect our salvation, but they do affect our rewards. Salvation is about our recognizing Christ's work for us; rewards are about God's recognizing our work for him.

What is life like in the present Heaven?

> *Revelation 6:9-11* . . . When the Lamb broke the fifth
> seal, I saw under the altar the souls of all who had
> been martyred for the word of God and for being
> faithful in their testimony. They shouted to the Lord
> and said, "O Sovereign Lord, holy and true, how
> long before you judge the people who belong to this
> world and avenge our blood for what they have done
> to us?" Then a white robe was given to each of them.
> And they were told to rest a little longer until the full
> number of their brothers and sisters—their fellow
> servants of Jesus who were to be martyred—had
> joined them.

These people in Heaven were the same ones killed
for Christ while on Earth. This demonstrates direct
continuity between our identity on Earth and our
identity in Heaven. People in Heaven will be remem-
bered for their lives on Earth. "They shouted to the
Lord" means they are able to express themselves audi-
bly. People in the intermediate Heaven can raise their
voices. This indicates they are rational, communicative,

and emotional—even passionate—beings, like people on Earth. The martyrs' wearing white robes suggests the possibility of actual physical forms, because disembodied spirits presumably don't wear robes. Those in Heaven are free to ask God questions, which means they have an audience with God. It also means they need to learn. In Heaven, people desire understanding and pursue it. There is also time in the present Heaven. People are aware of time's passing and are eager for the coming day of the Lord's judgment. God answers that they must "rest a little longer." Waiting requires the passing of time. I see no reason to believe that the realities of this passage apply only to one group of martyrs and to no one else in Heaven. We should assume that what is true of them is also true of our loved ones already there, and it will be true of us when we die.

Do Heaven's inhabitants remember life on Earth?

> *Revelation 6:9-10* . . . The souls of all who had
> been martyred . . . shouted to the Lord and said,
> "O Sovereign Lord, holy and true, how long before
> you judge the people who belong to this world and
> avenge our blood for what they have done to us?"

The martyrs depicted in Revelation 6 clearly remember at least some of what happened on Earth, including that they underwent great suffering. If they remember their martyrdom, there's no reason to think they would forget other aspects of their earthly lives. In fact, we'll all likely remember much more in Heaven than we do on Earth, and we will probably be able to see how God and angels intervened on our behalf even when we didn't realize it.

Memory is a basic element of personality. If we are truly ourselves in Heaven, there must be continuity of memory from Earth to Heaven. Heaven cleanses us but does not revise or extinguish our origins or our history. Undoubtedly we will remember God's works of grace in our lives that comforted, assured, sustained, and empowered us to live for him.

> *Luke 16:25* . . . Abraham said to him, "Son, remember that during your lifetime you had everything you wanted, and Lazarus had nothing. So now he is here being comforted, and you are in anguish."

Abraham calls upon the rich man, in Hell, to remember his life on Earth. Clearly he is capable of doing so; in fact, the context shows he remembers his brothers and the condition of their hearts, and he expresses his concern for them.

In Heaven, those who endured bad things on Earth, such as Lazarus, are comforted for them. This comfort implies a memory of what happened. If there were no memory of the bad things, what would be the need for or nature of such comfort?

> *2 Corinthians 5:10* . . . We must all stand before Christ to be judged. We will each receive whatever we deserve for the good or evil we have done in this earthly body.

Matthew 12:36 . . . I tell you this, you must give an account on judgment day for every idle word you speak.

After we die, we will give an account of our lives on Earth, down to specific actions and words. Certainly, we must remember the things we'll give an account for. Because we'll be held accountable for more than we presently remember, presumably our memory will be far better than it is now. The afterlife will not erase our memories; instead, it will enhance them.

Revelation 14:13 . . . I heard a voice from heaven saying, "Write this down: Blessed are those who die in the Lord from now on. Yes, says the Spirit, they are blessed indeed, for they will rest from their hard work; for their good deeds follow them!"

Matthew 6:19-21 . . . Don't store up treasures here on earth, where moths eat them and rust destroys them, and where thieves break in and steal. Store your treasures in heaven, where moths and rust cannot destroy, and thieves do not break in and steal. Wherever your treasure is, there the desires of your heart will also be.

God keeps a record in Heaven of what people, both unbelievers and believers, do on Earth. Our righteous deeds here will not be forgotten but will follow us to Heaven. The positions of authority and the treasures we're granted in Heaven will perpetually remind us of our lives on Earth, because God will take into account what we do on Earth in granting us those rewards.

Do people in the present Heaven see what is happening on Earth?

> *Revelation 6:9-10* . . . When the Lamb broke the fifth
> seal, I saw under the altar the souls of all who had
> been martyred for the word of God and for being
> faithful in their testimony. They shouted to the Lord
> and said, "O Sovereign Lord, holy and true, how long
> before you judge the people who belong to this world
> and avenge our blood for what they have done to us?"

If the martyrs in Heaven know that God hasn't yet
brought judgment on their persecutors, it seems evi-
dent that the inhabitants of the present Heaven can
see what's happening on Earth, at least to some extent.

> *Revelation 18:20* . . . Rejoice over her fate, O heaven
> and people of God and apostles and prophets! For at
> last God has judged her for your sakes.

When Babylon is brought down, an angel in Heaven
refers to events happening on Earth and speaks of them
to people living in Heaven. Clearly these inhabitants
of Heaven are aware of what's happening on Earth.

Revelation 19:1-2 . . . I heard what sounded like a
vast crowd in heaven shouting, "Praise the Lord!
Salvation and glory and power belong to our God.
His judgments are true and just. He has punished
the great prostitute who corrupted the earth with
her immorality. He has avenged the murder of
his servants."

Heaven's inhabitants are shown here praising God for
specific events of judgment that have just taken place on
Earth. Again, the saints in Heaven are clearly observing
what is happening on Earth. Those on Earth may be
ignorant of events in Heaven, but those in Heaven are *not*
ignorant of events on Earth, at least some of these events.

Luke 9:30-31 . . . Suddenly, two men, Moses and
Elijah, appeared and began talking with Jesus. They
were glorious to see. And they were speaking about
his exodus from this world, which was about to be
fulfilled in Jerusalem.

When called from Heaven to the Transfiguration on
Earth, Moses and Elijah seemed fully aware of the

drama they'd stepped into, of what was currently transpiring on Earth, and of God's redemptive plan about to be accomplished. That they were conversing with Jesus about his coming exodus from this world shows they had a far greater grasp of what was happening, and was about to happen, than his disciples did.

Revelation 3:15 . . . I know all the things you do, that you are neither hot nor cold. I wish that you were one or the other!

In Heaven, Christ watches closely what transpires on Earth, especially in the lives of God's people. If the sovereign God's attention is on Earth, why wouldn't the attention of his heavenly subjects be focused here as well? When a great war is transpiring, are those in the home country uninformed and unaware of it? When a great drama is taking place, do those who know the writer, producer, and cast—and have a great interest in the outcome—refrain from watching?

Luke 15:10 . . . There is joy in the presence of God's angels when even one sinner repents.

Notice this Scripture does not speak of rejoicing *by* the angels but *in the presence of* angels. Who is doing this rejoicing in Heaven? I believe it logically includes not only God but also the saints in Heaven, who would so deeply appreciate the wonder of human conversion—especially the conversion of those they knew and loved on Earth. If they rejoice over conversions happening on Earth, then obviously they must be *aware* of what's happening on Earth—and not just generally, but specifically, down to the details of specific individuals coming to faith in Christ.

Do people in Heaven pray for those on Earth?

> *Revelation 6:10* . . . [The martyrs] shouted to the Lord and said, "O Sovereign Lord, holy and true, how long before you judge the people who belong to this world and avenge our blood for what they have done to us?"

Based on the scriptural evidence, departed saints in the present Heaven do intercede in prayer—at least sometimes—for those of us still on Earth. The martyrs in Heaven pray, asking God to take specific action on Earth. They are praying for his justice on Earth, which has intercessory implications for Christians now suffering here.

If we believe that Heaven is a place of ignorance or disinterest about Earth, we will naturally assume that people in Heaven don't pray for people on Earth. However, if we believe that people in Heaven are aware of events on Earth and that they talk to God about his plan, his purpose, and his people, we will naturally assume they do pray for people on Earth. If prayer is simply talking to God, surely we will pray more in Heaven than we do now—not less.

Can it be Heaven if people are aware of anything bad on Earth?

Revelation 12:10-12 . . . I heard a loud voice shouting across the heavens, "It has come at last— salvation and power and the Kingdom of our God, and the authority of his Christ. For the accuser of our brothers and sisters has been thrown down to earth—the one who accuses them before our God day and night. And they have defeated him by the blood of the Lamb and by their testimony. And they did not love their lives so much that they were afraid to die. Therefore, rejoice, O heavens! And you who live in the heavens, rejoice! But terror will come on the earth and the sea, for the devil has come down to you in great anger, knowing that he has little time."

Luke 16:24-25 . . . The rich man shouted, "Father Abraham, have some pity! Send Lazarus over here to dip the tip of his finger in water and cool my tongue. I am in anguish in these flames." But Abraham said to him, "Son, remember that during your lifetime you had everything you wanted, and

> Lazarus had nothing. So now he is here being
> comforted, and you are in anguish."

Many maintain that those in Heaven cannot be aware of people and events on Earth because they would be made unhappy by all the suffering and evil; thus, Heaven would not truly be Heaven. I believe this argument is invalid. After all, God knows exactly what's happening on Earth, yet it doesn't diminish Heaven for him. Likewise, it's Heaven for the angels, even though they also know what's happening on Earth. In fact, angels in Heaven see the torment of Hell, but it doesn't negate their joy in God's presence. Abraham and Lazarus saw the rich man's agonies in Hell, but that didn't cause Paradise to cease to be Paradise. While this passage doesn't prove everyone in Heaven sees into Hell, it does suggest that God could allow this in some cases without diminishing his people's experience of Heaven.

> *Acts 9:4-5* . . . He fell to the ground and heard a voice
> saying to him, "Saul! Saul! Why are you persecuting

me?" "Who are you, lord?" Saul asked. And the voice replied, "I am Jesus, the one you are persecuting!"

Doesn't Christ's identifying himself with those being persecuted on Earth suggest he's currently hurting for his people, even though he's in Heaven? If Jesus, who is in Heaven, feels sorrow for his followers, might not others in Heaven grieve as well? It's one thing to no longer cry because there's nothing left to cry about, which will be true on the New Earth. But it's something else to no longer cry when there's still suffering on Earth. Going into the presence of Christ surely does not make us less compassionate.

Revelation 21:4 . . . He will wipe every tear from their eyes, and there will be no more death or sorrow or crying or pain. All these things are gone forever.

Christ's promise of no more tears or pain comes after the end of the old Earth, after the Great White Throne Judgment, after the old order of things has passed away and there's no more suffering on Earth. The present Heaven and the eternal Heaven are not the same. We can be assured there will be no more sorrow on the New Earth, our eternal home. But though the present Heaven is a far happier place than Earth under the Curse, Scripture doesn't state there can be no sorrow there. At the same time, people in Heaven are not frail beings whose joy can be preserved only by shielding them from what's really going on in the universe. Happiness in Heaven is not based on ignorance but on perspective.

Will we live in Heaven forever?

> *Isaiah 65:17* . . . Look! I am creating new heavens and a new earth, and no one will even think about the old ones anymore.

> *Revelation 21:2-4* . . . I saw the holy city, the new Jerusalem, coming down from God out of heaven like a bride beautifully dressed for her husband. I heard a loud shout from the throne, saying, "Look, God's home is now among his people! He will live with them, and they will be his people. God himself will be with them. He will wipe every tear from their eyes, and there will be no more death or sorrow or crying or pain. All these things are gone forever."

The answer to the question of whether we will live in Heaven forever depends on what we mean by "Heaven." Will we be with the Lord forever? Absolutely. Will we always be with him in exactly the same place that Heaven is now? No.

In the intermediate Heaven, we'll be in Christ's presence, and we'll be joyful, but we'll be looking forward to our bodily resurrection and permanent relocation to the New Earth. In Heaven, we'll await the time of Christ's return to Earth, our bodily resurrection, the final judgment, and the creation of the new heavens and New Earth.

In the context of Isaiah 65:17, God is not saying we will have no memory of life on the old Earth; he is saying, rather, that the former negative experiences of life here will not overshadow our happiness while living on the New Earth. Indeed, we will enjoy life on the New Earth far more because we won't forget what it was like to have lived under sin and the Curse and suffering. Warmth and light are most appreciated by people who remember what it was like to be cold and in the dark.

PART II

The Eternal Heaven

WHAT THE BIBLE SAYS ABOUT WHERE
WE WILL LIVE FOREVER

Where do we get our misconceptions about Heaven?

Isaiah 14:12-15 . . . How you are fallen from heaven, O shining star, son of the morning! You have been thrown down to the earth, you who destroyed the nations of the world. For you said to yourself, "I will ascend to heaven and set my throne above God's stars. I will preside on the mountain of the gods far away in the north. I will climb to the highest heavens and be like the Most High." Instead, you will be brought down to the place of the dead, down to its lowest depths.

John 8:44 . . . [Satan] was a murderer from the beginning. He has always hated the truth, because there is no truth in him. When he lies, it is consistent with his character; for he is a liar and the father of lies.

Revelation 13:6, NIV . . . [The beast] opened its mouth to blaspheme God, and to slander his name and his dwelling place and those who live in heaven.

The enemy of God slanders three things: God's person, God's people, and God's place—Heaven.

There's one central explanation for why so many of

God's children have such a vague, negative, and uninspired view of Heaven: Satan. After being forcefully evicted from Heaven, the devil became bitter not only toward God but toward mankind and toward Heaven itself, the place that was no longer his. It must be maddening for him that we're now entitled to the home from which he was evicted. What better way for the devil and his demons to attack us than to whisper lies about the very place on which God tells us to set our hearts and minds?

Some of Satan's favorite lies are about Heaven. Satan need not convince us that Heaven doesn't exist. He need only convince us that Heaven is a place of boring, unearthly existence. If we believe that lie, we'll be robbed of our joy and anticipation, we'll set our minds on this life and not the next, and we won't be motivated to share our faith. Fortunately, Jesus came here to the Shadowlands from the light of Heaven to tell us about his Father, the world beyond, and the world to come. If we listen to him—not the devil's lies—we will never be the same.

Is Heaven beyond our imagination?

2 Timothy 2:7 . . . Think about what I am saying. The Lord will help you understand all these things.

Psalm 119:18 . . . Open my eyes to see the wonderful truths in your instructions.

We can't anticipate or desire what we can't imagine. That's why God has given us glimpses of Heaven in the Bible—to fire our imaginations and kindle a desire for Heaven in our hearts. If God didn't want us to imagine what Heaven will be like, he wouldn't have told us as much about it as he has.

The writers of Scripture present Heaven in many ways, including as a garden, a city, and a kingdom. Because gardens, cities, and kingdoms are familiar to us, they afford us a bridge to understanding Heaven. However, many people make the mistake of assuming that these are merely analogies with no actual correspondence to the reality of Heaven (which would make them poor analogies). Analogies can be pressed too far, but because Scripture makes it clear that Jesus is preparing a place for us, that God's Kingdom will come to Earth, and that a physical resurrection awaits us, there is no reason to spiritualize or allegorize all earthly descriptions of Heaven. We should ask God's help to remove the blinders of our preconceived ideas about Heaven so we can understand Scripture.

If "no eye has seen" Heaven, how can we know about it?

> *1 Corinthians 2:9-10 . . .* "No eye has seen, no ear has heard, and no mind has imagined what God has prepared for those who love him." But it was to us that God revealed these things by his Spirit. For his Spirit searches out everything and shows us God's deep secrets.

> *Deuteronomy 29:29 . . .* The LORD our God has secrets known to no one. We are not accountable for them, but we and our children are accountable forever for all that he has revealed to us.

First Corinthians 2:9-10 is wonderful, but it says precisely the opposite of what it's cited to prove! What we otherwise could not have known, God says he has revealed to us through his Spirit. The context isn't talking about Heaven, but even if we apply these words to Heaven, they mean that God has revealed to us what it's like. Not exhaustively, but accurately.

God tells us about Heaven in his Word, not so

we can shrug our shoulders and remain ignorant, but because he wants us to understand and anticipate what awaits us. We should accept that many things about Heaven are secret and that God has countless surprises in store for us. But the things God *has* revealed to us about Heaven belong to us and to our children. It's critically important that we discuss and understand them.

Revelation 1:1-2 . . . This is a revelation from Jesus Christ, which God gave him to show his servants the events that must soon take place. He sent an angel to present this revelation to his servant John, who faithfully reported everything he saw. This is his report of the word of God and the testimony of Jesus Christ.

Isaiah 6:1-2 . . . It was in the year King Uzziah died that I saw the Lord. He was sitting on a lofty throne, and the train of his robe filled the Temple. Attending him were mighty seraphim, each having six wings. With two wings they covered their faces, with two they covered their feet, and with two they flew.

Ezekiel 1:1 . . . On July 31 of my thirtieth year, while I was with the Judean exiles beside the Kebar River in Babylon, the heavens were opened and I saw visions of God.

God commanded the apostle John to talk about his prolonged visit to Heaven, which he did in detail in the book of Revelation. Likewise, Isaiah and Ezekiel wrote about what they saw in Heaven. If God didn't intend for us to understand what he revealed to these men about Heaven, why would he bother telling us about it? When was the last time you wrote someone a letter using words you didn't expect them to comprehend? So, we should study, teach, and discuss God's revelation about Heaven given to us in his Word.

Is the eternal Heaven an actual place?

Revelation 21:10-11 ... He showed me the holy city, Jerusalem, descending out of heaven from God. It shone with the glory of God and sparkled like a precious stone—like jasper as clear as crystal.

Revelation 21:15-16 ... The angel who talked to me held in his hand a gold measuring stick to measure the city, its gates, and its wall. When he measured it, he found it was a square, as wide as it was long. In fact, its length and width and height were each 1,400 miles.

The New Earth and New Jerusalem are portrayed as actual places, with detailed physical descriptions.

John 14:2 ... There is more than enough room in my Father's home. If this were not so, would I have told you that I am going to prepare a place for you?

John 14:3 ... When everything is ready, I will come and get you, so that you will always be with me where I am.

Jesus uses ordinary, earthly, spatial terms to describe Heaven. If Heaven isn't a place, would Jesus have said it was? If we reduce Heaven to something less than or other than a place, we strip Christ's words of their meaning.

Is Heaven our default destination . . . or is Hell?

> *Matthew 7:13-14* . . . You can enter God's Kingdom only through the narrow gate. The highway to hell is broad, and its gate is wide for the many who choose that way. But the gateway to life is very narrow and the road is difficult, and only a few ever find it.

> *Romans 3:23* . . . Everyone has sinned; we all fall short of God's glorious standard.

> *Isaiah 59:2* . . . It's your sins that have cut you off from God.

Judging by what's said at most funerals, you'd think nearly everyone's going to Heaven. But Jesus made it clear that most people are not going to Heaven when he said the gateway to life is narrow and "only a few ever find it." Heaven is *not* our default destination. Because we are sinners, we are not entitled to enter God's presence. We cannot enter Heaven as we are. So unless our sin problem is resolved, the only place we will go is our true default destination . . . Hell.

Revelation 21:27 . . . Nothing evil will be allowed to enter, nor anyone who practices shameful idolatry and dishonesty—but only those whose names are written in the Lamb's Book of Life.

James 4:14 . . . How do you know what your life will be like tomorrow? Your life is like the morning fog— it's here a little while, then it's gone.

Joshua 24:15 . . . Choose today whom you will serve. . . . But as for me and my family, we will serve the LORD.

We dare not "wait and see" when it comes to what's on the other side of death. We shouldn't just cross our fingers and hope that our names are written in the Book of Life. We can know, we should know, before we die. And because we may die at any time, we need to know *now*—not next month or next year.

Is Hell real?

> *John 5:28-29* . . . Don't be so surprised! Indeed, the time is coming when all the dead in their graves will hear the voice of God's Son, and they will rise again. Those who have done good will rise to experience eternal life, and those who have continued in evil will rise to experience judgment.

> *Revelation 20:15* . . . Anyone whose name was not found recorded in the Book of Life was thrown into the lake of fire.

After Christ returns, there will be a resurrection of believers for eternal life in Heaven and a resurrection of unbelievers for eternal existence in Hell. It's common to deny or ignore the clear teaching of Scripture about Hell. To many, Hell seems to be disproportionate, a divine overreaction. But in fact it's arrogant that we, as creatures, would dare to take what we think is the high moral ground in opposition to what God the Creator has clearly revealed.

By denying the existence and endlessness of Hell,

we minimize Christ's work on the cross. Why? Because we lower the stakes of redemption. If Christ's crucifixion and resurrection didn't deliver us from an eternal Hell, his work on the cross is less heroic, less potent, less consequential, and thus less deserving of our worship and praise.

What did Jesus say about Hell?

> *Matthew 10:28* . . . Don't be afraid of those who want
> to kill your body; they cannot touch your soul. Fear
> only God, who can destroy both soul and body in hell.

> *Matthew 13:40–42* . . . Just as the weeds are sorted
> out and burned in the fire, so it will be at the end of
> the world. The Son of Man will send his angels, and
> they will remove from his Kingdom everything that
> causes sin and all who do evil. And the angels will
> throw them into the fiery furnace, where there will
> be weeping and gnashing of teeth.

> *Matthew 25:46* . . . [The cursed ones] will go away
> into eternal punishment, but the righteous will go
> into eternal life.

In the Bible, Jesus says more than anyone else about
Hell. He refers to it as a literal place and describes it
in graphic terms. Jesus taught that in Hell the wicked
suffer terribly, are fully conscious, retain their desires
and memories and reasoning, long for relief, cannot
be comforted, cannot leave their torment, and are

bereft of hope. The Savior could not have painted a bleaker picture.

In his book *The Problem of Pain*, C. S. Lewis writes of Hell, "There is no doctrine which I would more willingly remove from Christianity than this, if it lay in my power. But it has the full support of Scripture and, specifically, of our own Lord's words; it has always been held by Christendom; and it has the support of reason."

What will it mean to unite Heaven and Earth?

> *Ephesians 1:10* . . . This is the plan: At the right time
> he will bring everything together under the authority
> of Christ—everything in heaven and on earth.

Just as God and man will be forever united in Jesus,
so Heaven and Earth will forever be united in the
new physical universe, where we will live as resurrected beings. And just as the wall that separates
God and mankind is torn down in Jesus, the wall
that separates Heaven and Earth will also be forever
demolished.

> *Revelation 21:3* . . . I heard a loud shout from the
> throne, saying, "Look, God's home is now among
> his people! He will live with them, and they will
> be his people. God himself will be with them."

God's plan is to abolish the gulf between the spiritual and physical worlds. There will be no divided
loyalties or divided realms. There will be one cosmos,
one universe united under one Lord—forever. This is

the unstoppable plan of God. This is where history is headed. God will live with us on the New Earth. That will bring all things in Heaven and on Earth together.

Will the old Earth be destroyed . . . or renewed?

> *Luke 21:33* . . . Heaven and earth will disappear, but
> my words will never disappear.

> *2 Peter 3:10* . . . The day of the Lord will come
> as unexpectedly as a thief. Then the heavens will
> pass away with a terrible noise, and the very elements
> themselves will disappear in fire, and the earth and
> everything on it will be found to deserve judgment.

> *Revelation 21:1* . . . I saw a new heaven and a new
> earth, for the old heaven and the old earth had
> disappeared. And the sea was also gone.

At first glance, some Scriptures seem to suggest that
the earth will be utterly and permanently destroyed.
It's clear that the earth *as it is now* will not remain
forever—but what does that really mean?

> *Romans 8:19-23* . . . All creation is waiting eagerly for
> that future day when God will reveal who his children
> really are. Against its will, all creation was subjected
> to God's curse. But with eager hope, the creation

looks forward to the day when it will join God's children in glorious freedom from death and decay. For we know that all creation has been groaning as in the pains of childbirth right up to the present time. And we believers also groan, even though we have the Holy Spirit within us as a foretaste of future glory, for we long for our bodies to be released from sin and suffering. We, too, wait with eager hope for the day when God will give us our full rights as his adopted children, including the new bodies he has promised us.

This passage inseparably links the destinies of mankind and Earth. Our planet will be raised to new life in the same way that our bodies will be raised to new life.

1 Corinthians 3:13-14 . . . On the judgment day, fire will reveal what kind of work each builder has done. The fire will show if a person's work has any value. If the work survives, that builder will receive a reward.

Acts 3:21 . . . [Jesus] must remain in heaven until the time for the final restoration of all things, as God promised long ago through his holy prophets.

2 Corinthians 5:17 . . . Anyone who belongs to Christ
has become a new person. The old life is gone; a new
life has begun!

As we've seen in a number of passages that use words
such as *renewal* and *regeneration*, the same Earth destined for destruction is also destined for restoration.
Many have grasped the first teaching but not the second. Therefore, they misinterpret words such as *destroy*
to mean absolute and final destruction, rather than
what Scripture actually teaches: a temporary destruction that will be reversed through resurrection and
restoration.

In *The Bible and the Future*, Anthony Hoekema
writes, "If God would have to annihilate the present
cosmos, Satan would have won a great victory. Satan
would have succeeded in so devastatingly corrupting
the present cosmos and the present earth that God
could do nothing with it but blot it totally out of existence. But Satan did not win such a victory. On the
contrary, Satan has been decisively defeated. God will
reveal the full dimensions of that defeat when he shall

renew this very earth on which Satan deceived mankind and finally banish from it all the results of Satan's evil machinations."

God did not create matter to throw it away. God will regather all he needs of the scorched and disfigured Earth. Just as our old bodies will be raised to new bodies, the old Earth will be raised to become the New Earth. So, will the earth be destroyed or renewed? The answer is *both*—but the destruction will be temporary and partial, whereas the renewal will be eternal and complete.

Will the New Earth be familiar . . . like home?

> *Job 19:25-27* . . . I know that my Redeemer lives, and he will stand upon the earth at last. And after my body has decayed, yet in my body I will see God! I will see him for myself. Yes, I will see him with my own eyes.

> *1 Corinthians 13:12* . . . Now we see things imperfectly, like puzzling reflections in a mirror, but then we will see everything with perfect clarity. All that I know now is partial and incomplete, but then I will know everything completely, just as God now knows me completely.

A common misunderstanding about the eternal Heaven is that it will be unfamiliar. But that couldn't be further from the truth. When we hear that in Heaven we will have new bodies and live on a New Earth, this is how we should understand the word *new*—a restored and perfected version of our familiar bodies and our familiar Earth and our familiar relationships. Because we once lived on Earth, the New Earth will strike us as very familiar. A new car is a car, and a new friend is a friend. By calling it the New *Earth*, God emphatically tells us it will be earthly and, thus, familiar. If it won't be earthly, surely he wouldn't call it Earth.

> *Revelation 21:1*, NIV . . . I saw a new heaven and a new earth, for the first heaven and the first earth had passed away, and there was no longer any sea.

We're told the "first earth" will pass away. The Greek word for "first" is *prote*, suggesting a vital connection between the two earths. The first earth serves as the prototype or pattern for the New Earth. What we love about this life are the things that resonate with the life we were made for. The things we love are not merely the best this life has to offer—they are previews of the greater life to come. There's continuity between old and new. We should expect new trees, new flowers, new rocks, new rivers, new mountains, and new animals. As our current bodies are the blueprints for our resurrection bodies, this present Earth is the blueprint for the New Earth.

What will it mean to see God in Heaven?

> *Revelation 22:3-4* . . . The throne of God and of the
> Lamb will be there, and his servants will worship
> him. And they will see his face.

To see God's face is the loftiest of all aspirations—
though sadly, for most of us, it's not at the top of our
wish lists. (If we understood what it meant, it would be.)
To be told we'll see God's face is shocking to anyone who
understands God's transcendence and inapproachability.

> *Exodus 33:18-23* . . . Moses responded, "Then show
> me your glorious presence." The LORD replied, "I will
> make all my goodness pass before you, and I will call
> out my name, Yahweh, before you. . . . But you may
> not look directly at my face, for no one may see me
> and live." The LORD continued, "Look, stand near me
> on this rock. As my glorious presence passes by, I will
> hide you in the crevice of the rock and cover you with
> my hand until I have passed by. Then I will remove
> my hand and let you see me from behind. But my face
> will not be seen."

Moses saw God, but not God's face. To see God's face was utterly unthinkable. That's why, when we're told in Revelation 22:4 that we'll see God's face, it should astound us. For this to happen, it would require that we undergo something radical between now and then.

> *Hebrews 12:14* . . . Those who are not holy will not see the Lord.

It's only because we'll be fully righteous in Christ, completely sinless, that we'll be able to see God and live.

> *Job 19:25-27* . . . I know that my Redeemer lives, and he will stand upon the earth at last. And after my body has decayed, yet in my body I will see God! I will see him for myself. Yes, I will see him with my own eyes. I am overwhelmed at the thought!

Not only will we see his face and live, but we will likely wonder if we ever lived before we saw his face! To see God will be our greatest joy, the joy by which all others will be measured. To look into God's eyes will be to see what we've always longed to see: the person who made us for his own good pleasure.

Seeing God will be like seeing everything else for the first time. Why? Because not only will we see God, he will be the lens through which we see everything else—people, ourselves, and the events of this life.

> *Romans 1:20* . . . Ever since the world was created, people have seen the earth and sky. Through everything God made, they can clearly see his invisible qualities—his eternal power and divine nature.

> *2 Corinthians 3:18* . . . All of us who have had that veil removed can see and reflect the glory of the Lord. And the Lord—who is the Spirit—makes us more and more like him as we are changed into his glorious image.

We need not wait till the New Earth to catch glimpses of God. We're told that we "can clearly see his invisible qualities." Further, there will always be more to see when we look at God because his infinite character can never be exhausted. We could—and will—spend countless millennia exploring the depths of God's being and will be no closer to seeing it all than when we first started. This is the magnificence of God and the wonder of Heaven.

What will it mean for God to dwell among us?

> *Leviticus 26:11-12* . . . I will live among you, and I will not despise you. I will walk among you; I will be your God, and you will be my people.

> *Ezekiel 37:27* . . . I will make my home among them. I will be their God, and they will be my people.

The best part of life on the New Earth will be enjoying God's presence, having him actually dwell among us. God and mankind will be able to come to each other whenever they wish. To be with God—to know him, to see him—is the central, irreducible draw of Heaven.

> *2 Corinthians 6:16* . . . God said: "I will live in them and walk among them. I will be their God, and they will be my people."

> *Revelation 21:3* . . . I heard a loud shout from the throne, saying, "Look, God's home is now among his people! He will live with them, and they will be his people. God himself will be with them."

God will actually come to live among us on the New Earth. God's Son didn't become a man temporarily, but permanently. His incarnation will last forever, and his throne—and hence his home—will be on the New Earth. We will not have to leave home to visit God, nor will God leave home to visit us. In the new universe, we'll never be able to travel far enough to leave God's presence. Even if we could, we'd never want to.

> *Revelation 21:22* . . . I saw no temple in the city, for the Lord God Almighty and the Lamb are its temple.

There will be no temple. Everyone will be allowed unimpeded access into God's presence.

> *Hebrews 11:16* . . . They were looking for a better place, a heavenly homeland. That is why God is not ashamed to be called their God, for he has prepared a city for them.

> *Revelation 22:14* . . . Blessed are those who wash their robes. They will be permitted to enter through the gates of the city and eat the fruit from the tree of life.

Not only will God come to dwell with us on Earth, he will also bring with him the New Jerusalem, an entire city of people, structures, streets, walls, rivers, and trees that is now in the present Heaven. Just as the Holy of Holies contained the dazzling presence of God in ancient Israel, so the New Jerusalem will contain his presence—but on a much larger scale—on the New Earth. We will be able to come physically, through wide open gates, to God's throne.

Will God serve us?

> *Isaiah 25:6* . . . In Jerusalem, the LORD of Heaven's
> Armies will spread a wonderful feast for all the people
> of the world. It will be a delicious banquet with clear,
> well-aged wine and choice meat.

If God's serving us were our idea, it would be blasphemy. But it's *his* idea. As husbands serve their wives and parents serve their children, God desires to serve us. In Heaven, God will overwhelm us with his humility and grace.

> *John 13:8* . . . "No," Peter protested, "you will never
> ever wash my feet!" Jesus replied, "Unless I wash you,
> you won't belong to me."

Even though we don't deserve it, we must assent to Christ's service for us because if we don't allow him to give us what we need, we can't really be his.

> *Matthew 20:28* . . . Even the Son of Man came not to
> be served but to serve others and to give his life as a
> ransom for many.

Luke 12:37 . . . The servants who are ready and waiting for his return will be rewarded. I tell you the truth, he himself will seat them, put on an apron, and serve them as they sit and eat!

We will be in Heaven only because "the Son of Man came not to be served but to serve others and to give his life as a ransom for many." But even in Heaven, it appears, Jesus will sometimes serve us. What greater and more amazing experience could be ours in the new universe than to have Jesus choose to serve us?

How will we worship God in Heaven?

> *Revelation 5:13* . . . I heard every creature in heaven
> and on earth and under the earth and in the sea.
> They sang: "Blessing and honor and glory and power
> belong to the one sitting on the throne and to the
> Lamb forever and ever."

Most people know that we'll worship God in Heaven.
But they don't grasp how thrilling that will be.
Multitudes of God's people—of every nation, tribe,
people, and language—will gather to sing praise to
God for his greatness, wisdom, power, grace, and
mighty work of redemption.

> *Revelation 5:14* . . . The four living beings said,
> "Amen!" And the twenty-four elders fell down and
> worshiped the Lamb.

> *Revelation 7:11* . . . All the angels were standing
> around the throne and around the elders and the four
> living beings. And they fell before the throne with
> their faces to the ground and worshiped God.

In Heaven, where everyone worships Jesus, no one says, "Now we're going to sing two hymns, followed by announcements and prayer." The singing isn't ritual but spontaneous praise. Overwhelmed by his magnificence, we will fall on our faces to worship with unrestrained happiness.

> *Revelation 7:9, 12* . . . I saw a vast crowd, too great to count, from every nation and tribe and people and language, standing in front of the throne and before the Lamb. . . . They sang, "Amen! Blessing and glory and wisdom and thanksgiving and honor and power and strength belong to our God forever and ever! Amen."

We are created to worship God. There's no higher pleasure. At times we'll lose ourselves in praise, doing nothing but worshiping him. At other times we'll worship him when we build a cabinet, paint a picture, cook a meal, talk with an old friend, take a walk, or throw a ball. In Heaven, worshiping God won't be restricted to a time posted on a sign, telling us when to start and stop. It will permeate our lives, energize our bodies, and fuel our imaginations.

Will we actually rule with Christ in Heaven?

> *1 Corinthians 6:2-3* . . . Don't you realize that
> someday we believers will judge the world? . . .
> Don't you realize that we will judge angels?

The form of the verb in this question implies that we won't simply judge angels a single time but will continually rule them. Paul addresses the subject of God's people one day ruling the world as if it were Theology 101, as though it's something everyone should know. (Yet when I teach on this, many Christians appear to have never heard it.)

> *Psalm 72:8, 11* . . . May he reign from sea to sea, and
> from the Euphrates River to the ends of the earth.
> . . . All kings will bow before him, and all nations will
> serve him.

> *Revelation 22:5* . . . There will be no night there—
> no need for lamps or sun—for the Lord God will
> shine on [his servants]. And they will reign forever
> and ever.

God created Adam and Eve to be king and queen over the earth. Their job was to rule the earth in righteousness, to the glory of God. They failed. Jesus Christ is the second and last Adam, and the church is his bride, the second Eve. Christ is king, the church is his queen. Christ will exercise dominion over all nations of the earth. As the new head of the human race, Christ—with his beloved people as his bride and corulers—will at last accomplish what was entrusted to Adam and Eve. God's saints will fulfill on the New Earth the role God first assigned to Adam and Eve on the old Earth.

Revelation 2:10 . . . If you remain faithful even when facing death, I will give you the crown of life.

Revelation 4:10 . . . The twenty-four elders fall down and worship the one sitting on the throne (the one who lives forever and ever). And they lay their crowns before the throne.

Revelation 3:11 . . . I am coming soon. Hold on to what you have, so that no one will take away your crown.

Because crowns are the primary symbol of ruling, every mention of crowns as rewards is a reference to our ruling with Christ.

> *Matthew 25:23* . . . The master said, "Well done, my good and faithful servant. You have been faithful in handling this small amount, so now I will give you many more responsibilities."

> *Luke 16:10* . . . If you are faithful in little things, you will be faithful in large ones.

God is grooming us for leadership. He's watching us to see how we demonstrate our faithfulness. He does that through his apprenticeship program, one that prepares us for Heaven. Christ is not simply preparing a place for us; he is preparing us for that place. If we serve faithfully on the present Earth, God will give us permanent management positions on the New Earth.

How will we rule God's Kingdom?

> *Daniel 7:27* . . . The sovereignty, power, and greatness
> of all the kingdoms under heaven will be given to the
> holy people of the Most High. His kingdom will last
> forever, and all rulers will serve and obey him.

Not only does God give pleasures to us as his heirs, he also gives us power—positions of authority in his eternal Kingdom. Our vested interest in the New Earth couldn't be greater. The New Earth isn't a blissful realm that we'll merely visit, as vacationers go to a theme park. Rather, it's a realm we'll joyfully rule with Jesus, exercising dominion as God's image bearers.

The Kingdom will be God's, yet he will appoint his saints as rulers under him, and they "will serve and obey him." What is the "greatness of all the kingdoms under heaven" that will be "given to the holy people of the Most High"? It includes all that makes the nations great. That would consist of, among other things, their cultural, artistic, athletic, scientific, and intellectual achievements. All these will not be lost or destroyed but "given to the holy people of the Most High" as they rule God's eternal Kingdom on the New Earth. We will become the stewards, or managers, of the world's wealth and accomplishments, all for God's glory.

> *Genesis 1:26-28* . . . God said, "Let us make human beings in our image, to be like us. They will reign over the fish in the sea, the birds in the sky, the livestock, all the wild animals on the earth, and the small animals that scurry along the ground." So God created human beings in his own image. In the image of God he created them; male and female he created them. Then God blessed them and said, "Be fruitful and multiply. Fill the earth and govern it. Reign over the fish in the sea, the birds in the sky, and all the animals that scurry along the ground."

One day, we will do exactly what God originally designed us to do—rule the earth as his righteous representatives.

Shouldn't we be excited that God will reward us by making us rulers in his Kingdom? God's intention for humans is that we would occupy the whole earth and reign over it. This dominion would produce God-exalting societies in which we would exercise the creativity, imagination, intellect, and skills befitting beings created in God's image, thereby manifesting his attributes.

PART III

Life on the New Earth

A topical guide to our many questions
about the eternal Heaven

Abilities

Will our new bodies have new abilities?

John 20:19 . . . The disciples were meeting
behind locked doors because they were afraid of
the Jewish leaders. Suddenly, Jesus was standing there
among them!

Luke 24:31 . . . Suddenly, their eyes were opened,
and they recognized him. And at that moment
he disappeared!

Acts 1:9 . . . He was taken up into a cloud while they
were watching, and they could no longer see him.

Philippians 3:21 . . . He will take our weak mortal
bodies and change them into glorious bodies like his
own, using the same power with which he will bring
everything under his control.

Christ's resurrection body had an ability to appear
suddenly, apparently coming through a locked door to
the apostles. And "he disappeared" from the sight of

the two disciples at Emmaus. When Christ left the earth, he defied gravity and ascended into the air. It's possible that the risen Christ, who is man yet God, has certain physical abilities we won't have. Appearing and disappearing could be a limited expression of his omnipresence, and his ascension might be something our bodies couldn't imitate.

On the one hand, because we're told in multiple passages that our resurrection bodies will be like Christ's, it may be possible at times for us to transcend the present laws of physics and/or travel in some way we're not now capable of. On the other hand, it's our God-given human nature to be embodied creatures existing in space and time. So it's likely that the same laws of physics that governed Adam and Eve will govern us. We can't be sure, but either way it will be wonderful.

1 Corinthians 15:53 . . . Our dying bodies must be transformed into bodies that will never die; our mortal bodies must be transformed into immortal bodies.

Our resurrection bodies will never fail us. They'll work in perfect concert with our resurrected minds. We won't get sick, grow old, or die from either an accident or natural causes.

Age

Will we all appear the same age?

> *Isaiah 11:6-9* . . . In that day the wolf and the lamb
> will live together; the leopard will lie down with the
> baby goat. The calf and the yearling will be safe with
> the lion, and a little child will lead them all. . . . The
> baby will play safely near the hole of a cobra. Yes,
> a little child will put its hand in a nest of deadly snakes
> without harm. . . . For as the waters fill the sea, so the
> earth will be filled with people who know the LORD.

The theologian Thomas Aquinas said we will all be the same age as Jesus when he died, about thirty-three. But the Bible doesn't give a definite answer. I do believe that on the New Earth many opportunities lost in this life will be wonderfully restored. Perhaps children who died young will be allowed to have the childhood they never had, and their parents will receive the joy of watching them grow. Perhaps we'll see people as we remember them most on Earth. Or perhaps we'll see them as ageless.

Regardless of what age we appear, our bodies will demonstrate the qualities of youthfulness that Jesus so valued in children—curiosity, gratefulness, a longing to learn and explore, and eagerness to hear stories and gather close to loved ones.

Alien Life

Will we find new beings on other worlds?

> *Isaiah 65:17*, NIV . . . Behold, I will create new heavens
> and a new earth.

No Scripture passage proves that God will or will not create new races of intelligent beings, either on Earth or on other planets spread across the new universe. It's not speculative, however, to say there will be a new celestial universe of stars and planets. Scripture is clear on this point; that's what "new heavens" means. Whether God might inhabit them with new creatures is not provable but certainly possible.

Some people say, "To imagine that God would populate worlds with new beings is just science fiction." We may have it backward. Science fiction is the result of mankind's God-given sense of adventure, wonder, creativity, and imagination. It emerges from being made in God's image. It's not our sinfulness that arouses that excitement. It's our God-given hunger for adventure, for new realms and new beings, for new beauties and new knowledge.

God has given us a longing for new worlds. Considering that his higher glory and praise come not from inanimate objects such as stars and planets but from intelligent beings such as people and angels, it's no great stretch to suppose he might create other intelligent beings. It's up to him, not us. But won't it be fun to find out?

Angels

Will we become angels?

> *Hebrews 1:14* . . . Angels are only servants—spirits sent to care for people who will inherit salvation.

> *Daniel 10:13* . . . Michael, one of the archangels, came to help me, and I left him there with the spirit prince of the kingdom of Persia.

> *Revelation 12:7* . . . There was war in heaven. Michael and his angels fought against the dragon and his angels.

Angels are angels. Humans are humans. Angels are beings with their own histories and memories, with distinct identities reflected in the fact that they have personal names, such as Michael and Gabriel. Under God's direction, they serve us on Earth. Michael, the archangel, serves under God; and the other angels, in various positions, serve under Michael.

> *1 Corinthians 6:2-3* . . . Don't you realize that someday we believers will judge the world? And since you are

going to judge the world, can't you decide even these
little things among yourselves? Don't you realize that
we will judge angels?

On the New Earth, human beings will govern angels.
Perhaps the same angels who serve God now by watching out for us in this life will be under our leadership
then. If so, imagine the stories they'll have to tell us!

2 Corinthians 5:8 . . . Yes, we are fully confident, and
we would rather be away from these earthly bodies,
for then we will be at home with the Lord.

Death is a relocation of the same person from one place
to another. The place changes, but the person remains
the same. The same person who becomes absent from
his or her body becomes present with the Lord. We
won't become angels, but we'll be with angels—and
that'll be far better.

Animals

Will animals inhabit the New Earth?

> *Isaiah 11:6-8* . . . In that day the wolf and the lamb
> will live together; the leopard will lie down with the
> baby goat. The calf and the yearling will be safe with
> the lion, and a little child will lead them all. The cow
> will graze near the bear. The cub and the calf will
> lie down together. The lion will eat hay like a cow.
> The baby will play safely near the hole of a cobra.
> Yes, a little child will put its hand in a nest of deadly
> snakes without harm.

> *Isaiah 65:17, 25* . . . Look! I am creating new heavens
> and a new earth. . . . The wolf and the lamb will feed
> together. . . . In those days no one will be hurt or
> destroyed on my holy mountain. I, the LORD, have
> spoken!

Scripture says a great deal about animals, portraying
them as Earth's second-most important inhabitants.
God entrusted animals to us, and our relationships
with animals are a significant part of our lives. These

descriptions of animals peacefully inhabiting the earth may have application to a millennial kingdom on the old Earth, but their primary reference appears to be to God's eternal Kingdom, where mankind and animals will together enjoy a redeemed Earth.

How will people and animals relate?

> *Genesis 2:18-19* . . . The LORD God said, "It is not good for the man to be alone. I will make a helper who is just right for him." So the LORD God formed from the ground all the wild animals and all the birds of the sky. He brought them to the man to see what he would call them, and the man chose a name for each one.

> *Psalm 8:6-8* . . . You gave [human beings] charge of everything you made, putting all things under their authority—the flocks and the herds and all the wild animals, the birds in the sky, the fish in the sea, and everything that swims the ocean currents.

> *Proverbs 12:10* . . . The godly care for their animals, but the wicked are always cruel.

God created us to be stewards of animals. He holds us accountable for how we treat them. We needn't speculate how God might populate a perfect earth. He populated Eden with animals, under the rule of people.

God doesn't make mistakes. There's every reason to believe he'll restore this self-proclaimed "very good" arrangement on the New Earth. We should expect the New Earth to be a place where we'll fulfill our calling to be faithful rulers and stewards of animals.

Might some animals talk in Heaven?

> *Genesis 3:1* . . . The serpent was the shrewdest of
> all the wild animals the LORD God had made.
> One day he asked the woman, "Did God really say
> you must not eat the fruit from any of the trees in
> the garden?"

The "shrewdest of all the wild animals" suggests that some of the other animals were also shrewd. Animals were smart, probably smarter than we imagine; the most intelligent animals we see around us are but fallen remnants of what once was. Today Satan can speak through a human being but not an animal because people can talk and animals can't. But the fact that he spoke through an animal in Eden suggests the animals had the capacity to speak. There's no indication Eve was surprised to hear an animal speak, which suggests other animals also may have spoken. Even today whales, dolphins, elephants, and birds, as well as various primates, make sounds that communicate specific and sometimes detailed messages to their own kind. Might they originally have had even greater communicative abilities?

> *Revelation 8:13* . . . I looked, and I heard a single eagle crying loudly as it flew through the air, "Terror, terror, terror to all who belong to this world because of what will happen when the last three angels blow their trumpets."

> *Revelation 5:13* . . . I heard every creature in heaven and on earth and under the earth and in the sea. They sang: "Blessing and honor and glory and power belong to the one sitting on the throne and to the Lamb forever and ever."

Just because these passages are in the book of Revelation doesn't mean they can't be literal. When the serpent spoke to Eve and when the donkey spoke to Balaam (Numbers 22:28-30), the stories are recorded as historical narrative, not as apocalyptic literature. Nothing in the context of the Genesis account or the Balaam story indicates these shouldn't be taken literally. If people will be smarter and more capable on the New Earth, should it surprise us that animals might also be smarter and more capable? Might their restored or enhanced abilities include communication understandable to humans?

Will animals praise God?

> *Psalm 148:7, 10-13* . . . Praise the LORD from the earth, you . . . wild animals and all livestock, small scurrying animals and birds, kings of the earth and all people, rulers and judges of the earth, young men and young women, old men and children. Let them all praise the name of the LORD. For his name is very great; his glory towers over the earth and heaven!

> *Revelation 5:13* . . . I heard every creature in heaven and on earth and under the earth and in the sea. They sang: "Blessing and honor and glory and power belong to the one sitting on the throne and to the Lamb forever and ever."

Throughout Scripture we read that animals praise God. I don't know exactly how animals praise God, but our inability to understand it shouldn't keep us from believing it. If in some sense fallen animals, shadows of what they once were, can praise God on this fallen Earth, how much more should we expect them to do so on the New Earth?

> *Revelation 4:8-9*, NIV . . . Each of the four living creatures had six wings and was covered with eyes all around, even under his wings. Day and night they never stop saying: "Holy, holy, holy is the Lord God Almighty, who was, and is, and is to come." . . . The living creatures give glory, honor and thanks to him who sits on the throne.

The Greek word translated "living creatures" is *zoon*. Throughout most of the New Testament, that word is translated "animal." In virtually every case inside and outside of Scripture, *zoon* means not a person, not an angel, but an animal. Although earthly animals aren't capable of verbalizing praise as these animals in Heaven do, the passages speaking of earthly animals praising God and the story of Balaam's donkey clearly suggest that animals have a spiritual dimension far beyond our understanding. The Bible tells us that animals, in their own way, praise God. By extending to them the blessings of mankind's redemption, just as he extended to them the curses of mankind's sin, God may well grant animals an important role on the New Earth.

Will extinct animals live on the New Earth?

> *Revelation 21:5,* esv . . . Behold, I am making all
> things new.

> *Genesis 1:24-25* . . . God said, "Let the earth produce
> every sort of animal, each producing offspring of
> the same kind—livestock, small animals that scurry
> along the ground, and wild animals." And that is
> what happened. God made all sorts of wild animals,
> livestock, and small animals, each able to produce
> offspring of the same kind. And God saw that it
> was good.

God spoke to Job of the Creator's magnificence seen in
two great ancient creatures, Behemoth and Leviathan
(Job 40–41).

Were dinosaurs part of God's original creation of
a perfect animal world? Certainly. Will the restoration of Earth and the redemption of God's creation be
complete enough to bring back extinct animals? Will
extinct animals be included in the "all things" Christ
will make new? There's every reason to think so and no

persuasive argument against it. We should fully expect that extinct animals and plants will be brought back to life.

By resurrecting most of his original creation, God could show the totality of his victory over sin and death. Animals were created for God's glory. What could speak more of his awesome power than a tyrannosaurus? Imagine Jurassic Park with all the awesome majesty of those huge creatures but none of their violence and hostility. Imagine riding a brontosaurus—or flying on the back of a pterodactyl. Unless God made a mistake when he originally created them—and clearly he didn't—why *wouldn't* he include them when he makes "all things new"?

Anticipation

How can I change my perspective so that I truly look forward to Heaven?

> *Luke 6:21* . . . God blesses you who weep now, for in due time you will laugh.

> *Luke 15:10* . . . There is joy in the presence of God's angels when even one sinner repents.

Nobody wants to leave a good party early. Christians faced with death often feel they're leaving the party before it's over. They have to go home early. They're disappointed, thinking of all they'll miss when they leave.

But the truth is, the real party is under way at home—precisely where they're going! They're not the ones missing the party; those of us left behind are. (Fortunately, if we know Jesus, we'll get there eventually to join the party.)

One by one, believers will disappear from the world. Those of us who are left behind will grieve that our loved ones have left home. In reality, however, our believing loved ones aren't leaving home, they're going home. They'll be home before us. We'll be arriving at the party a little later. Laughter and rejoicing—a party awaits us. Don't you want to join it?

Yet even that party, in the present Heaven, is a preliminary celebration. To be in resurrected bodies on a resurrected Earth in resurrected friendships, enjoying the resurrected culture with the resurrected Jesus—now that will be the ultimate party! We will all be who God made us to be—and none of us will ever suffer or die again. As a Christian, the day I die will be the best day I've ever lived. But it won't be the best day I ever will live. Resurrection day will be far better. And the first day on the New Earth—that will be one big step for mankind, one giant leap for God's glory.

Bodies

Will we all have beautiful bodies?

> *Revelation 5:9* . . . [Jesus'] blood has ransomed people for God from every tribe and language and people and nation.

> *Revelation 7:9* . . . I saw a vast crowd, too great to count, from every nation and tribe and people and language, standing in front of the throne and before the Lamb.

Racial identities will continue in Heaven, and this involves a genetic carryover from the old body to the new. No doubt we'll be recognizable to one another. But we'll be healthy and attractive, untouched by the Curse or disease or restrictions, and we'll each be perfectly happy with the form God designed for us.

Our resurrection bodies will be free of the curse of sin, redeemed, and restored to their original beauty and purpose that goes back to Eden. The only bodies we've ever known are weak and diseased remnants of the original bodies God made for humans. But the bodies we'll have on the New Earth, after our resurrection, will be even more glorious than those of Adam and Eve. The most beautiful person you've ever seen is under the Curse, a shadow of the beauty that once characterized humanity. But in the Resurrection, the sinless beauty of the inner person will overflow into the beauty of the outer person. Of this we can be certain— no matter what we will look like, our bodies will please the Lord, ourselves, and others.

Will our resurrection bodies have five senses?

2 Corinthians 5:3 . . . We will put on heavenly bodies; we will not be spirits without bodies.

Philippians 3:20-21 . . . The Lord Jesus Christ . . . will take our weak mortal bodies and change them into glorious bodies like his own, using the same power with which he will bring everything under his control.

We'll stand on the New Earth and see it, feel it, smell it, taste its fruits, and hear its sounds. Not figuratively. Literally. We know this because we're promised resurrection bodies like Christ's. He saw and heard and felt, and when he cooked and ate fish after his resurrection, no doubt he smelled and tasted it. We will too. God designed us with five senses. They're part of what makes us human. Because God's original ideas are always good, our resurrection bodies will surely have these senses. And for all we know, they may have more.

Psalm 139:14 . . . Thank you for making me so wonderfully complex! Your workmanship is marvelous—how well I know it.

If our current bodies are so marvelous, as David recognizes, how much more will we praise God for the wonders of our resurrection bodies? Will our eyes be able to function alternately as telescopes and microscopes? Will our eyes be able to see new colors? Will our ears serve as sound-gathering disks? Will our sense of smell be far more acute, able to identify a favorite flower—or person—miles away, so we can follow the scent to the source?

Although we don't know the answers to these questions, it seems reasonable to suggest all of our resurrected senses will function at levels we've never known. On the New Earth, we'll continually be discovering, to our delight, what we never knew existed, what we've been missing all our lives. No joy is greater than the joy of discovery. The God who always surpasses our expectations will forever give us more of himself and his creation to discover.

Books and Reading

Will there be books in Heaven?

> *Psalm 119:89* . . . Your eternal word, O Lord, stands firm in heaven.

> *Matthew 24:35* . . . Heaven and earth will disappear, but my words will never disappear.

We know that sixty-six books—those that comprise the Bible—will be in Heaven, because they will last forever.

> *Revelation 20:12* . . . I saw the dead, both great and small, standing before God's throne. And the books were opened, including the Book of Life. And the dead were judged according to what they had done, as recorded in the books.

> *Psalm 56:8* . . . You keep track of all my sorrows. You have collected all my tears in your bottle. You have recorded each one in your book.

There are also other books in Heaven. The books spoken of in Revelation 20 contain detailed historical records of the lives of all of us on this earth. The book mentioned specifically is the Book of Life, in which the names of God's people are written. There's no indication that these books will be destroyed.

> *Revelation 5:1* . . . I saw a scroll in the right hand of the one who was sitting on the throne. There was writing on the inside and the outside of the scroll, and it was sealed with seven seals.

> *Revelation 10:2* . . . In his hand was a small scroll that had been opened. He stood with his right foot on the sea and his left foot on the land.

These passages describe scrolls in Heaven. Jesus opens a great scroll, and an angel holds a little scroll.

> *Malachi 3:16-18* . . . Those who feared the LORD spoke with each other, and the LORD listened to what they said. In his presence, a scroll of remembrance was written to record the names of those who feared

> him and always thought about the honor of his name.
> "They will be my people," says the LORD of Heaven's
> Armies. . . . "You will again see the difference
> between the righteous and the wicked, between those
> who serve God and those who do not."

God is proud of his people for fearing him and honoring his name. He promises that one day all will plainly see the differences between those who serve him and those who don't. Those distinctions are documented in this scroll in Heaven.

The king often had scribes record the deeds of his subjects so that he could remember and properly reward his subjects' good deeds (Esther 6:1-11). While God needs no reminder, he makes a permanent record, probably kept near his throne, so that the entire universe will one day know the basis on which he has rewarded the righteous and punished the wicked.

Boredom

Will Heaven ever be boring?

Revelation 13:5-6 . . . The beast was allowed to speak . . . terrible words of blasphemy against God, slandering his name and his dwelling.

Genesis 2:15–17; 3:4–7, 17, 23 . . . The LORD God placed the man in the Garden of Eden. . . . But the LORD God warned him, "You may freely eat the fruit of every tree in the garden—except the tree of the knowledge of good and evil. If you eat its fruit, you are sure to die." . . . "You won't die!" the serpent [said] to the woman. "God knows that your eyes will be opened as soon as you eat it, and you will be like God, knowing both good and evil." The woman was convinced. She saw that the tree was beautiful and its fruit looked delicious, and she wanted the wisdom it would give her. So she took some of the fruit and ate it. Then she gave some to her husband, who was with her, and he ate it, too. At that moment their eyes were opened, and they suddenly felt shame at their nakedness. . . . To the man [the Lord] said, "Since you listened to your wife and ate from the tree whose fruit I commanded you not to eat, the ground is cursed because of you. All your life you will struggle to scratch a living from it." . . . So the Lord God banished them from the Garden of Eden, and he sent Adam out to cultivate the ground from which he had been made.

Sadly, even among Christians, it's a prevalent myth that Heaven will be boring. Sometimes we can't envision anything beyond strumming a harp and polishing streets of gold. Satan's most basic strategy, the same one he employed with Adam and Eve, is to make us believe that sin brings fulfillment. However, in reality, sin robs us of fulfillment. Sin doesn't make life interesting; it makes life empty. Sin doesn't create adventure; it blunts it. Sin doesn't expand life; it shrinks it. Sin's emptiness inevitably leads to boredom. When there's fulfillment, when there's beauty, when we see God as he truly is—an endless reservoir of fascination—boredom becomes impossible.

Psalm 16:11 . . . You will show me the way of life, granting me the joy of your presence and the pleasures of living with you forever.

Everything good, enjoyable, refreshing, fascinating, and interesting is derived from God. Without God, there's nothing interesting to do. God promises that we'll laugh, rejoice, and experience endless pleasures in Heaven. To be in his presence will be the very opposite of boredom. Once we're with the Lord, the only boring place in the universe will be Hell.

Clothing

Will we wear clothes?

> *Revelation 6:11* . . . A white robe was given to each of [the martyrs].

It appears we'll wear clothes, not because there will be shame or temptation, but perhaps because they will enhance our appearance and comfort. Wearing robes might strike us as foreign or formal. But to first-century readers, robes were just normal, and anything but robes would have seemed strange. Rather than conclude that we'll all wear robes, a better deduction may be that we'll all dress normally, as we did on the old Earth in our particular culture.

> *Revelation 7:9* . . . I saw a vast crowd . . . standing in front of the throne and before the Lamb. They were clothed in white robes.

White clothes may depict our righteousness, as they did Christ's in his transfiguration (Matthew 17:2).

The emphasis on white may relate to cleanliness, which was extremely hard to maintain in that culture. This passage doesn't teach that we will always wear the same thing.

> *Revelation 15:6* . . . The seven angels . . . were clothed in spotless white linen with gold sashes across their chests.

Will white be the only clothing color? No. There are golden sashes. Because resurrected people retain their individuality and nationality and because many ethnic groups wear colorful clothing, we should expect this on the New Earth.

Conflict

Will we ever disagree in Heaven?

> *Ephesians 2:6-7* . . . [God] raised us from the dead along with Christ and seated us with him in the heavenly realms because we are united with Christ Jesus. So God can point to us in all future ages as examples of the incredible wealth of his grace and kindness toward us, as shown in all he has done for us who are united with Christ Jesus.

Because we're finite and unique and because we'll never know everything, we may not agree about everything in Heaven. We'll agree on innumerable matters and wonder how we ever thought otherwise. But we'll still likely have different tastes in food and clothes and music and thousands of other things.

Likely we will have discussions, perhaps even debates, about things we won't yet understand. Some will have insights others don't. Some will have a better understanding in one area, others in a different area. Our beliefs can be accurate but incomplete, because we'll not be omniscient. Uniqueness and differences existed before sin and will exist after it. Only God has infinite wisdom and knowledge. We should expect some differences in perspective, but we should also expect an ability to resolve them without rancor or bruised egos.

Imagine the ability to question and challenge without any malice and to be questioned and challenged without a hint of defensiveness. Wouldn't that be Heaven?

Culture

Will ancient cultures be resurrected to the New Earth?

> *Revelation 21:26* . . . All the nations will bring their
> glory and honor into the city.

There will be not one nation but many. This reference gives us biblical basis to suppose that the best of each culture—the history, art, music, and languages of the old Earth—will be redeemed, purified, and carried over to the New Earth.

> *Daniel 7:27* . . . The sovereignty, power, and greatness
> of all the kingdoms under heaven will be given to the
> holy people of the Most High.

Surely the greatness of the nations that will be handed over to God's people cannot be restricted only to those nations existing at Christ's return. Do you have a special interest in Europe of the Middle Ages? Then perhaps you'll enjoy developing relationships with those who lived in that era. It's likely we'll not merely meet the redeemed people of ancient civilizations but also walk among redeemed civilizations. Because there is a continuity in the resurrection of the dead, we have every reason to believe that people will not become just the same but will carry over their God-glorifying distinctives from the old Earth to the new.

Desires

Will we have desires in Heaven?

> *Hebrews 8:10* . . . This is the new covenant I will make
> with the people of Israel on that day, says the LORD:
> I will put my laws in their minds, and I will write
> them on their hearts.

God placed just one restriction on Adam and Eve in Eden, and when they disregarded it, the universe unraveled. On the New Earth, God will no longer put that test before us. God's law, the expression of his attributes, will be written on our hearts. No rules will be needed, for our hearts will be given over to God. What we should do will at last be identical with what we want to do.

> *Psalm 37:4* . . . Take delight in the LORD, and he will
> give you your heart's desires.

Desire is an essential part of humanity, a part that God built into people before sin cast its dark shadow on

Earth. We'll have many desires in Heaven, but they won't be unholy desires. Everything we want will be good. Our desires will please God. When we delight in God and abide in him, whatever we want will be exactly what he wants for us.

Emotions

Will we have emotions?

> *Revelation 21:4* ... He will wipe every tear from their
> eyes, and there will be no more death or sorrow or
> crying or pain.

This verse primarily addresses the tears coming from injustice and sorrow, not tears per se. Hence, we might shed tears of joy in Heaven. Can you imagine joy flooding your eyes as you meet Christ and as you're reunited with loved ones? Regardless, we know there will be no more tears of grief because there will be no more reason for grief.

> *Revelation 6:10* ... [The martyrs] shouted to the
> Lord and said, "O Sovereign Lord, holy and true,
> how long before you judge the people who belong to
> this world and avenge our blood for what they have
> done to us?"

> *Revelation 7:11* ... All the angels were standing
> around the throne and around the elders and the four

living beings. And they fell before the throne with
their faces to the ground and worshiped God.

In Heaven we'll exercise not only intellect but also
emotions. Even angels respond emotionally. Emotions
are part of our God-created humanity, not sinful bag-
gage to be destroyed. We should anticipate pure and
accurately informed emotions guided by reality. Our
present emotions are skewed by sin, but one day they'll
be delivered from it.

> *Luke 6:21* . . . God blesses you who are hungry now,
> for you will be satisfied. God blesses you who weep
> now, for in due time you will laugh.

We know that people in Heaven have lots of feelings—all good ones. We're told of banquets, feasts,
and singing. People will laugh. Feasting, singing, and
rejoicing involve feelings. Feelings aren't part of the
Curse; they're part of how God made human beings
from the beginning. Our present emotions are bent by
sin, but they will be forever straightened when God
removes the Curse.

Entertainment and Recreation

Will we play in Heaven?

> *Mark 10:14-15* . . . When Jesus saw what was
> happening, he was angry with his disciples. He said
> to them, "Let the children come to me. Don't stop
> them! For the Kingdom of God belongs to those who
> are like these children. I tell you the truth, anyone
> who doesn't receive the Kingdom of God like a child
> will never enter it."

When we were children, we played—with one another
and with dogs and cats and frogs. We enjoyed hiding,
climbing trees, sledding, and throwing snowballs and
baseballs. We played without having to stop to earn
a living. We played just because it was fun. Is God
pleased by that? Yes, because he created and values a
childlike spirit.

Will we dance?

Exodus 15:20 . . . Miriam the prophet, Aaron's sister, took a tambourine and led all the women as they played their tambourines and danced.

2 Samuel 6:16 . . . As the Ark of the LORD entered the City of David, Michal, the daughter of Saul, looked down from her window . . . [and] saw King David leaping and dancing before the LORD.

Luke 15:25-27 . . . The older son was in the fields working. When he returned home, he heard music and dancing in the house, and he asked one of the servants what was going on. "Your brother is back," he was told, "and your father has killed the fattened calf. We are celebrating because of his safe return."

Throughout the ages, people have danced to God's glory on Earth. After the parting of the Red Sea, Miriam and the women of Israel danced and played tambourines, singing praises to God. King David leaped and danced and celebrated before the Lord. When the Prodigal Son returned, the house was filled with music and dancing. How much more should we expect to dance on the New Earth?

As music is a means of worship, so is dancing. Unfortunately, many popular forms of dancing have become associated with immorality and immodesty. But, of course, those kinds of dancing won't exist on the New Earth. It's God, not Satan, who made us to dance, and we can all look forward to dancing on the New Earth.

Equality

Will all people be equal in Heaven?

> *Proverbs 22:2* . . . The rich and poor have this in common: The LORD made them both.

> *Acts 10:34-35* . . . God shows no favoritism. In every nation he accepts those who fear him and do what is right.

> *1 Corinthians 12:14-17* . . . The body has many different parts, not just one part. If the foot says, "I am not a part of the body because I am not a hand," that does not make it any less a part of the body. And if the ear says, "I am not part of the body because I am not an eye," would that make it any less a part of the body? If the whole body were an eye, how would you hear? Or if your whole body were an ear, how would you smell anything?

All people are equal in worth, but they differ in gifting and function. There's no reason to believe we'll all be equally tall or strong or that we'll have the same gifts, talents, or intellectual capacities. If we all had the same gifts, they wouldn't be special. If everyone were equal in Heaven in all respects, it would mean we'd have no role models, no heroes, no one to look up to, no thrill of learning from someone we consider wiser than ourselves.

God is the creator of diversity, and diversity involves inequality of gifting. Because God promises to reward people differently according to their differing degrees of faithfulness in this life, we should not expect equality of possessions and positions in Heaven. But there will be no jealousy or arrogance concerning our differences.

Family

Will there be family in Heaven?

> *Luke 8:21* . . . Jesus [said], "My mother and my
> brothers are all those who hear God's word and
> obey it."

> *Mark 10:29-30* . . . [Jesus said,] "I assure you that
> everyone who has given up house or brothers or
> sisters or mother or father or children or property,
> for my sake and for the Good News, will receive now
> in return a hundred times as many houses, brothers,
> sisters, mothers, children, and property. . . . And in
> the world to come that person will have eternal life."

We'll have family relationships with people who were
our blood family on Earth. But we'll also have family relationships with our friends, both old and new.
Resurrection bodies will presumably have chromosomes and DNA, with a signature that forever testifies
to our genetic connection with our earthly family. But
what Jesus was saying is that devotion to God creates a

bond transcending biological family ties. Heaven won't be without families but will be one big family, in which all family members are friends and all friends are family members.

Many of us treasure our families. But many others have endured a lifetime of broken hearts stemming from twisted family relationships. In Heaven neither we nor our family members will cause pain. Our relationships will be harmonious—what we've always longed for.

Food and Drink

Will we eat and drink?

> *John 21:12-14* . . . "Come and have some
> breakfast!" Jesus said. None of the disciples dared
> to ask him, "Who are you?" They knew it was the
> Lord. Then Jesus served them the bread and the
> fish. This was the third time Jesus had appeared
> to his disciples since he had been raised from
> the dead.

> *Philippians 3:21* . . . He will take our weak mortal
> bodies and change them into glorious bodies like his
> own, using the same power with which he will bring
> everything under his control.

Jesus proved that resurrection bodies are capable of
eating food, real food. He could have abstained from
eating. The fact that he didn't is a powerful statement
about the nature of his resurrection body, and by impli-
cation, ours, because Christ will transform our lowly
bodies into "glorious bodies like his own."

Luke 22:29-30 . . . Just as my Father has granted me a Kingdom, I now grant you the right to eat and drink at my table in my Kingdom.

Revelation 2:7 . . . To everyone who is victorious I will give fruit from the tree of life in the paradise of God.

Luke 22:18 . . . [Jesus said,] "I will not drink wine again until the Kingdom of God has come."

Matthew 8:11 . . . Many Gentiles will come from all over the world—from east and west—and sit down with Abraham, Isaac, and Jacob at the feast in the Kingdom of Heaven.

Scripture contains many figures of speech. But it's incorrect to assume that because some figures of speech are used to describe Heaven, all of what the Bible says about Heaven is figurative. Because we're told we'll have resurrection bodies like Christ's and that he ate in his resurrection body, we should not conclude he was speaking figuratively when he refers to tables, banquets, and eating and drinking in his Kingdom.

How will food taste in Heaven?

> *Isaiah 25:6* . . . In Jerusalem, the Lord of Heaven's
> Armies will spread a wonderful feast for all the people
> of the world. It will be a delicious banquet with clear,
> well-aged wine and choice meat.

Our resurrected bodies will have resurrected taste buds.
We can trust that the food we eat on the New Earth,
some of it familiar and some of it brand new, will taste
better than anything we've ever eaten here. The best
meals we will ever eat await us on the New Earth.

Free Will

Will we have free will in Heaven?

> *Romans 5:18-19* . . . Adam's one sin brings condemnation for everyone, but Christ's one act of righteousness brings a right relationship with God and new life for everyone. Because one person disobeyed God, many became sinners. But because one other person obeyed God, many will be made righteous.

Some people believe that if we have free will in Heaven, we'll have to be free to sin, as were the first humans. But Adam and Eve's situation was different. They were innocent but had not been made righteous *by Christ*. We, on the other hand, become righteous through Christ's atonement. To suggest we could have Christ's righteousness yet sin is to say Christ could sin. Adam and Eve had a capacity for sin, just as we do now, but when we're with God, we'll no longer have that capacity.

Once we become what the sovereign God has

made us to be in Christ and once we see him as he is, then we'll see all things—including sin—for what they are. God won't need to restrain us from sin. It will have absolutely no appeal. It will be, literally, unthinkable. The inability to sin doesn't inherently violate free will. God cannot sin, yet no being has greater free choice than God. We will forever choose freely *and* rightly.

Friendships

Who will our friends be in Heaven?

> *Acts 17:26*, NIV . . . From one man [God] made every nation of men, that they should inhabit the whole earth; and he determined the times set for them and the exact places where they should live.

Because God determined the time and exact places where you would live, it's no accident which neighborhood you grew up in, who lived next door, who went to school with you, who was part of your church youth group, who was there to help you and pray for you. Our relationships were appointed by God, and there's every reason to believe they'll continue in Heaven. Friendships begun on Earth will continue in Heaven, becoming richer than ever.

> *Matthew 8:11* . . . Many Gentiles will come from all over the world—from east and west—and sit down with Abraham, Isaac, and Jacob at the feast in the Kingdom of Heaven.

Jesus told us we'll sit at the dinner table with Abraham, Isaac, and Jacob. If we sit with them, we should expect to sit with others. What do people do at feasts? In Middle Eastern culture, dinner was—and is—not only about good food and drink but also about building relationships, talking together, and telling stories.

Perhaps you're disappointed that you've never had the friendships you long for. In Heaven you'll have much closer relationships with some people you now know, but it's also true that you may never have met the closest friends you'll ever have. Just as someone may be fifty years old before meeting her best friend, you may live on the New Earth enjoying many friendships before meeting someone who will become your dearest friend. Or, maybe your best friend will be someone you've never before met, sitting next to you at the first great feast.

Gender

Will we still be male or female?

> *Genesis 1:27* . . . God created human beings in his
> own image. In the image of God he created them;
> male and female he created them.

> *John 20:14-16* . . . [Mary Magdalene] turned to leave
> and saw someone standing there. It was Jesus, but
> she didn't recognize him. . . . She thought he was the
> gardener. "Sir," she said, "if you have taken him away,
> tell me where you have put him, and I will go and get
> him." "Mary!" Jesus said. She turned to him and cried
> out, "Rabboni!" (which is Hebrew for "Teacher").

Was Jesus genderless after his resurrection? Of course
not. No one mistook him for a woman or as androgy-
nous. He's called "Sir" and referred to with male pro-
nouns. Moses and Elijah, when they appeared with
Christ, were recognized as two men (Luke 9:30).
Human bodies aren't genderless. The point of bodily
resurrection is that we will have real human bodies

essentially linked to our original ones. Gender is a God-created aspect of humanity. It is an essential part of who we are. In the final Resurrection, women will be women and men will be men.

Hell

If our loved ones are in Hell, won't that spoil Heaven?

> *Romans 1:19-20* . . . [Sinful people] know the truth
> about God because he has made it obvious to them.
> For ever since the world was created, people have
> seen the earth and sky. Through everything God
> made, they can clearly see his invisible qualities—
> his eternal power and divine nature. So they have
> no excuse for not knowing God.

In Heaven we'll see clearly that God revealed himself to
each person and that he gave opportunity for each heart
or conscience to seek and respond to him. We will know
that God was merciful and his final judgment was fair.

> *1 John 2:2* . . . He himself is the sacrifice that atones
> for our sins—and not only our sins but the sins of all
> the world.

> *Matthew 7:13* . . . You can enter God's Kingdom
> only through the narrow gate. The highway to hell
> is broad, and its gate is wide for the many who choose
> that way.

Everyone deserves Hell. No one deserves Heaven. Jesus went to the cross to offer salvation to all because God doesn't desire any to perish, yet many will perish in their unbelief. So even if God offered mercy, what consolation will that be to us if our loved ones refused to receive it?

I believe that in a sense, none of our loved ones will be in Hell—only some whom we *once* loved. Our love for our companions in Heaven will be directly linked to God, the central object of our love. We will see him in them. We will not love those in Hell because when we see Jesus as he is, we will love only—and will only want to love—whoever and whatever pleases and glorifies and reflects him.

What we loved in those who died without Christ was God's beauty we once saw in them. When God forever withdraws from them, I think it's likely they'll no longer bear his image and no longer reflect his beauty. Without God, they'll be stripped of all the qualities we loved. Therefore, paradoxically, they will not truly be the people we loved. I can't prove biblically what I've just stated, but it rings true to me, even if the thought now seems horrifying.

Homes

Will we have our own homes?

> *John 14:2*, NIV . . . In my Father's house are many
> rooms. . . . I am going there to prepare a place for you.

This verse suggests that Jesus has in mind for each
of us an individual dwelling that's a smaller part of a
larger place. This place will be home to us in the most
unique sense.

> *Isaiah 65:17, 21* . . . I am creating new heavens and
> a new earth. . . . In those days people will live in
> the houses they build and eat the fruit of their own
> vineyards.

> *Luke 16:9*, NIV . . . Use worldly wealth to gain friends
> for yourselves, so that when it is gone, you will be
> welcomed into eternal dwellings.

Heaven isn't likely to have lots of identical residences.
God loves diversity, and he custom-tailors his children and his provisions for them. When we see the

particular places he's prepared for us—not just for mankind in general but for each of us in particular—we'll rejoice to see our ideal home. We'll be free to build on it and develop it as we see fit, to God's glory. Our love for home, our yearning for it, is a glimmer of our longing for our true home.

Identity

Will we be ourselves in Heaven?

Luke 24:39 . . . [Jesus said,] "Look at my hands. Look at my feet. You can see that it's really me."

John 20:16 . . . "Mary!" Jesus said. She turned to him and cried out, "Rabboni!" (which is Hebrew for "Teacher").

John 20:27-28 . . . [Jesus] said to Thomas, "Put your finger here, and look at my hands. Put your hand into the wound in my side. Don't be faithless any longer. Believe!" "My Lord and my God!" Thomas exclaimed.

John 21:12-15 . . . "Now come and have some breakfast!" Jesus said. None of the disciples dared to ask him, "Who are you?" They knew it was the Lord. Then Jesus served them the bread and the fish. This was the third time Jesus had appeared to his disciples since he had been raised from the dead. After breakfast Jesus asked Simon Peter, "Simon son of

John, do you love me more than these?" "Yes, Lord,"
Peter replied, "you know I love you."

The resurrected Jesus did not become someone else; he remained who he was before his resurrection. In John's Gospel, Jesus deals with Mary, Thomas, and Peter in very personal ways, drawing on his previous knowledge of them. His knowledge and relationships from his pre-resurrected state carried over to his resurrected state.

> *Isaiah 66:22* . . . "As surely as my new heavens
> and earth will remain, so will you always be my
> people, with a name that will never disappear,"
> says the Lord.

> *Matthew 26:29* . . . [Jesus said,] "Mark my
> words—I will not drink wine again until the day
> I drink it new with you in my Father's Kingdom."

These verses speak of the present "you" maintaining the same identity in the future. You will be *you* in Heaven. Who else would you be? If Bob, a man on Earth, is no longer Bob when he gets to Heaven, then, in fact, Bob did not go to Heaven. If we weren't ourselves in the afterlife, then we couldn't be held accountable for what we did in this life. The Judgment would be meaningless. Our own personal history and identity will endure from one Earth to the next. We'll be ourselves without the sin—meaning that we'll be the best we can be.

> *Luke 16:25* . . . Abraham said to [the rich man in the place of the dead], "Son, remember that during your lifetime you had everything you wanted, and Lazarus had nothing. So now he is here being comforted."

Jesus called people in Heaven by name, including Lazarus in the intermediate Heaven and Abraham, Isaac, and Jacob in the eternal Heaven (Matthew 8:11). A name denotes a distinct identity, an individual. The fact that people in Heaven can be called by the same name they had on Earth demonstrates they remain the same people.

> *Luke 24:39* . . . [Jesus said,] "Look at my hands. Look at my feet. You can see that it's really me. Touch me

and make sure that I am not a ghost, because ghosts
don't have bodies, as you see that I do."

Job 19:26-27, NIV . . . After my skin has been destroyed,
yet in my flesh I will see God; I myself will see him
with my own eyes—I, and not another. How my heart
yearns within me!

If you know Jesus, you'll be you in Heaven—without
the bad parts—forever.

Will we be unique in Heaven?

> *Matthew 8:11* . . . Many Gentiles will come from all
> over the world—from east and west—and sit down
> with Abraham, Isaac, and Jacob at the feast in the
> Kingdom of Heaven.

We'll sit at a banquet and eat with Abraham and Isaac
and others. That means we will be sitting and eating
beside, talking with, and laughing with not merely a
general assembly, but particular individuals.

> *Luke 15:7* . . . There is more joy in heaven over one lost
> sinner who repents and returns to God than over ninety-
> nine others who are righteous and haven't strayed away!

Heaven's inhabitants don't rejoice over nameless
multitudes coming to God. They rejoice over each
and every person. That's a powerful affirmation of
Heaven's view of each person as a separate individual
whose life is observed and cared for one at a time.
Individuality was God's plan from the beginning. Just
as our genetic code and fingerprints are unique now,
we should expect the same of our new bodies.

Will we have ethnic and national identities?

> *Revelation 5:9-10* . . . You are worthy. . . . Your
> blood has ransomed people for God from every
> tribe and language and people and nation. And
> you have caused them to become a Kingdom
> of priests for our God. And they will reign on
> the earth.

Who will serve as the New Earth's kings and priests? Not people who were *formerly* of every tribe, language, people, and nation, but people who will continue to be. Their distinctions aren't obliterated but continue into the intermediate Heaven and then into the eternal Heaven.

Tribe refers to a person's clan and family lineage. *People* refers to race. *Nation* refers to those who share a national identity and culture. Will we have ethnic and national identities? Yes. Hundreds of nations, thousands of people groups will gather to worship Christ. And many national and cultural distinctives, untouched by sin, will continue to the glory of God. The kings and leaders of nations will be united because they share the King's righteousness; and they, with him, will rejoice in their differences as a tribute to his creativity and multifaceted character.

Knowledge and Learning

Will we know everything in Heaven?

> *1 Peter 1:12*, NIV . . . Even angels long to look into these things.

> *1 Corinthians 13:12* . . . Now we see things imperfectly, like puzzling reflections in a mirror, but then we will see everything with perfect clarity. All that I know now is partial and incomplete, but then I will know everything completely, just as God now knows me completely.

Righteous angels don't know everything, and they long to know more. They're flawless but finite. In Heaven we'll be flawless, but not knowing everything isn't a flaw. It's part of being finite. God alone is omniscient. The point of comparing our knowing to God's knowing is that we'll know fully, in the sense of accurately but not exhaustively. When we die, we'll see things far more clearly and we'll know much more than we do now, but we'll *never* know everything. We should expect to long for greater knowledge, as angels do. And we'll spend eternity gaining the greater knowledge we'll seek.

I frequently learn new things about my wife, daughters, and closest friends, even though I've known them for many years. If I can always be learning something new about finite, limited human beings, surely I'll learn far more about Jesus. None of us will ever begin to exhaust his depths.

Will we learn in Heaven?

> *Ephesians 2:6-7,* NIV . . . God raised us up with Christ
> and seated us with him in the heavenly realms in
> Christ Jesus, in order that in the coming ages he
> might show the incomparable riches of his grace.

The word *show* means "to reveal." The phrase *in the coming ages* clearly indicates this will be a progressive, ongoing revelation, in which we learn more and more about God's grace.

> *Revelation 21:5* . . . The one sitting on the throne
> said, "Look, I am making everything new!"

After creating the new universe, Jesus says, "I am making everything new!" Notice the verb tense is not "I have made" or "I will make" but "I am making." This suggests an ongoing process of renovation. Christ is a creator, and his creativity is never exhausted.

> *Luke 2:52* . . . Jesus grew in wisdom and in stature and
> in favor with God and all the people.

Hebrews 5:8 . . . Even though Jesus was God's Son, he learned obedience from the things he suffered.

Nothing is wrong with process and the limitations it implies. Jesus "grew in wisdom and in stature." Jesus "learned obedience." Growing and learning cannot be bad; the sinless Son of God experienced them. They are simply part of being human. Unless we cease to be human after our bodily resurrection, we will go on growing and learning.

2 Corinthians 3:18 . . . The Lord—who is the Spirit— makes us more and more like him as we are changed into his glorious image.

When we enter Heaven, we'll presumably begin with the knowledge we had at the time of our death. God may enhance our knowledge and will likely correct countless wrong perceptions. I imagine he'll reveal many new things to us, then set us on a course of continual learning, paralleling Adam and Eve's. We won't ever know everything, and even what we will know, we won't know all at once.

Will our knowledge and skills vary? Will some people in Heaven have greater knowledge and specialized abilities than others? Why not? Scripture shows there will be differences in Heaven. We will be individuals, each with our own memories and God-given gifts. Some of our knowledge will overlap, but not all. We'll be learners forever. God doesn't want us to stop learning. What he wants to stop is what prevents us from learning.

Landmarks

Will places on the present Earth be resurrected to the New Earth?

> *Matthew 19:28* . . . Jesus [said], "I assure you that when the world is made new and the Son of Man sits upon his glorious throne, you who have been my followers will also sit on twelve thrones, judging the twelve tribes of Israel."

> *2 Corinthians 5:17* . . . Anyone who belongs to Christ has become a new person. The old life is gone; a new life has begun!

In becoming new, will the old Earth retain much of what it once was? The New Earth will still be just as much Earth as the new us will still be us. Shouldn't we expect, then, that some of the same geological features of the old Earth will characterize the new? Shouldn't we expect the New Earth's sky to be blue? Might God refashion the rain forests or the Grand Canyon? If the earth becomes the New Earth, might Lake Louise become the New Lake Louise?

Might we travel to a familiar place and say, "This is the very spot we stood on," in the same sense that we'll be able to say, "These are the very hands I used to help the needy"? C. S. Lewis calls this world Shadowlands, a copy of something that once was, Eden, and also that will be, the New Earth. On the New Earth we will see the *real* Earth, which includes the good things not only of God's natural creation but also of mankind's creative expression to God's glory. On the New Earth, no good thing will be destroyed. I believe all of the old Earth that matters will be drawn into Heaven, to be part of the New Earth.

Languages

What languages will we speak?

> *Revelation 7:10, NIV* . . . They cried out in a
> loud voice.

This singular "voice" implies a shared language. This could be a trade language, Heaven's equivalent to Swahili or English, second languages that many know in addition to their native languages, allowing them to communicate. Or the common language could be our primary one. It may be a universal language God grants us without our having to learn it. If he wishes, God could allow us to understand all languages even if we can't speak them.

> *Genesis 11:1, 4-7* . . . At one time all the people of
> the world spoke the same language and used the
> same words. . . . Then they said, "Come, let's build
> a great city for ourselves with a tower that reaches
> into the sky. This will make us famous and keep
> us from being scattered all over the world." But
> the LORD came down to look at the city and the

tower the people were building. "Look!" he said. "The people are united, and they all speak the same language. After this, nothing they set out to do will be impossible for them! Come, let's go down and confuse the people with different languages. Then they won't be able to understand each other."

The Babel account offers clues to the importance of shared language in an ideal society. God confused the language of the people and dispersed them, so their great city went unfinished. Notice that all people originally shared one language, which empowered them to cooperate together in great achievements. But because they were united in self-glorification rather than God-glorification, they embraced a false unity that would've empowered further rebellion and self-destruction. Because the people weren't united around their God-designed purpose to rule the earth for his glory, God removed a source of their destructive unity and power—their shared language. Once mankind is made righteous and entrusted with stewarding the New Earth, God will likely restore a common language.

Laughter and Fun

Will we laugh in Heaven?

> *Luke 6:23*, NIV . . . Rejoice in that day and
> leap for joy, because great is your reward
> in heaven.

Just as Jesus promises satisfaction as a reward in Heaven, he also promises laughter as a reward. Anticipating the laughter to come, Jesus says we should leap for joy now. Can you imagine someone leaping for joy in utter silence, without laughter? Take any group of rejoicing people, and what do you hear? Laughter. If God didn't have a sense of humor, we as his image bearers wouldn't. It is God's gift to humanity, a gift that will be raised to new levels after our bodily resurrection.

> *Luke 6:21* . . . God blesses you who are
> hungry now, for you will be satisfied. God
> blesses you who weep now, for in due time
> you will laugh.

The reward of those who mourn now will be laughter later. I'm convinced Christ will laugh with us, and his wit and fun-loving nature will be our greatest source of endless laughter.

Marriage

Will there be marriage?

> *Matthew 22:30* . . . When the dead rise, they will
> neither marry nor be given in marriage. In this
> respect they will be like the angels in heaven.

> *Ephesians 5:31-32* . . . The Scriptures say, "A man
> leaves his father and mother and is joined to his
> wife, and the two are united into one." This is a
> great mystery, but it is an illustration of the way
> Christ and the church are one.

The Bible appears to say that human marriage as we
now know it will not exist after the final Resurrection
(Matthew 22:30). However, Scripture does *not* teach
there will be no marriage in Heaven. In fact, it makes
clear there *will* be marriage in Heaven. What it says is
that there will be *one* marriage, between Christ and his
bride—and we'll all be part of it.

The one-flesh marital union we know on Earth is
a signpost pointing to our relationship with Christ as

our bridegroom. Once we reach the destination, the signpost becomes unnecessary. That one marriage—our marriage to Christ—will be so completely satisfying that even the most wonderful earthly marriage couldn't be as fulfilling.

Many happily married people are troubled by this, but they shouldn't be. Christ never suggested that deep relationships between married people will end. I fully expect that my wife, Nanci, and I will be closer friends than ever. We will remember fondly the lives we forged together on the old Earth, the children and grandchildren we had. All of us together will forever be part of the same marriage, an eternal marriage to Jesus, our bridegroom.

Music

Will we sing and make music in Heaven?

> *Psalm 104:33*, NIV . . . I will sing to the LORD all my life; I will sing praise to my God as long as I live.

> *1 Chronicles 25:6* . . . All these men were under the direction of their fathers as they made music at the house of the LORD. Their responsibilities included the playing of cymbals, harps, and lyres at the house of God.

> *Psalm 150:3-6* . . . Praise him with a blast of the ram's horn; praise him with the lyre and harp! Praise him with the tambourine and dancing; praise him with strings and flutes! Praise him with a clash of cymbals; praise him with loud clanging cymbals. Let everything that breathes sing praises to the LORD! Praise the LORD!

On Earth, creative, artistic, and skilled people sing and play instruments to glorify God. The Bible is full of examples of people praising God with singing and with musical instruments. There's every reason to believe that on the New Earth we will do the same.

> *Revelation 8:7, 13* . . . The first angel blew his trumpet. . . . Then I looked, and I heard . . . , "Terror, terror, terror to all who belong to this world because of what will happen when the last three angels blow their trumpets."

> *Revelation 14:3* . . . This great choir sang a wonderful new song in front of the throne of God.

> *Revelation 15:2-3* . . . I saw before me what seemed to be a glass sea mixed with fire. And on it stood all the people who had been victorious over the beast and his statue and the number representing his name. They were all holding harps that God had given them. And they were singing the song of Moses, the servant of God, and the song of the Lamb.

The apostle John speaks of trumpets and harps in the present Heaven. If we'll have musical instruments in our pre-resurrected state, how much more should we expect to find them on the New Earth? The 144,000 "who had been redeemed from the earth" sing a "new song" before God's throne (Revelation 14:3). People in Paradise sing a "song of Moses," a song written on the fallen Earth—likely the song of Exodus 15, rejoicing in the redemption of Passover. This suggests we'll sing both old and new songs, songs written on Earth and songs written in Heaven.

Nature

Will the New Earth be an Eden-like Paradise?

> *Genesis 2:8-9* . . . The LORD God planted a garden in Eden in the east, and there he placed the man he had made. The LORD God made all sorts of trees grow up from the ground—trees that were beautiful and that produced delicious fruit. In the middle of the garden he placed the tree of life and the tree of the knowledge of good and evil.

> *John 14:2-3* . . . [Jesus said,] "There is more than enough room in my Father's home. If this were not so, would I have told you that I am going to prepare a place for you? When everything is ready, I will come and get you, so that you will always be with me where I am."

The phrase "planted a garden" shows God's personal touch, his intimate interest in the creative details of mankind's home on Earth. God poured himself, his creativity, and his love into making Eden for his creatures. But at that time, that's all we were: his creatures, his image bearers. Now that we are both his children and his bride, chosen to live with him forever, would we expect to live in a place more or less than Eden? More, of course. And that's exactly what the New Earth will be. This world, even under the Curse, gives us foretastes and glimpses of the next world.

> *Isaiah 55:13* . . . Where once there were thorns, cypress trees will grow. Where nettles grew, myrtles will sprout up. These events will bring great honor to the LORD's name; they will be an everlasting sign of his power and love.

> *Ezekiel 36:35* . . . People will say, "This former wasteland is now like the Garden of Eden! The abandoned and ruined cities now have strong walls and are filled with people!"

Just like the Garden of Eden, the New Earth will be a place of sensory delight, breathtaking beauty, satisfying relationships, and personal joy. If Christ prepared Eden so carefully and lavishly for mankind in the six days of Creation, what has he fashioned in the place he's been preparing for us in the two thousand years since he left this world? It won't be a non-Eden; it will be a renovated and glorified Eden, with the tree of life right in the middle.

What will new nature be like?

> *Isaiah 35:1* . . . Even the wilderness and desert will
> be glad in those days. The wasteland will rejoice and
> blossom with spring crocuses.

We've never seen men and women as they were intended to be. Likewise, we've never seen nature unchained and undiminished. We've only seen it cursed and decaying. Yet even now we behold a great deal that pleases and excites us, moving our hearts to worship. If the "wrong side" of Heaven can be so beautiful, what will the "right side" look like? If the smoking remains are so stunning, what will Earth look like when it's resurrected and made new, restored to the original but even better?

> *Isaiah 51:3* . . . The LORD will comfort Israel
> again and have pity on her ruins. Her desert
> will blossom like Eden, her barren wilderness
> like the garden of the LORD. Joy and gladness
> will be found there. Songs of thanksgiving will
> fill the air.

The earthly beauty we see now won't be lost. We won't trade Earth's beauty for Heaven's; Earth's beauty will gain even deeper beauty. As we will live forever with the people of this world—redeemed—we will enjoy forever the beauties of this world—redeemed.

Will the New Earth have new and unique natural wonders?

> *Revelation 21:10* . . . He took me in the Spirit to
> a great, high mountain, and he showed me the
> holy city, Jerusalem, descending out of heaven
> from God.

Because it will be called the New Earth, we should expect geographical properties of Earth: mountains, waterfalls, and other natural wonders. Just as our resurrection bodies will be better than our current ones, the New Earth's natural wonders will presumably be more spectacular than those we now know. We can expect more magnificent mountains and more beautiful lakes and flowers than those on this earth. If we imagine the New Earth to have fewer and less beautiful features than the old, we picture the Earth's regression. But in fact, there's every reason to anticipate *progression*. Everything God tells us suggests we will look back at the present Earth and conclude that it was God's creative beginning, and his creativity will never end.

Hebrews 12:28 . . . Since we are receiving a Kingdom that is unshakable, let us be thankful and please God by worshiping him with holy fear and awe.

Some current earthly phenomena may not occur on the New Earth, including earthquakes, floods, hurricanes, and volcanoes. These may be aberrations due to the Curse. However, it may be that the foundations of the New Earth's buildings will be such that they would remain solid in the most violent storms or earthquakes. And certainly God could easily arrange for his people to be in the right place at the right time, so that what we now call accidents won't happen. In that case, we might ride out an earthquake as if we were on a roller coaster—experiencing the thrill of the event without the danger. We could praise God for the display of his magnificent power.

Will there be no more sunsets?

> *Revelation 22:5* . . . There will be no night there—no need for lamps or sun—for the Lord God will shine on [his servants].

Some people believe this is figurative, speaking of the moral perfection of the New Earth. Darkness is associated with crime, evil done under the cover of night. Yet darkness isn't evil—God created it before the Fall. Night is also associated with positive things: time with family after a hard day's work; opportunities to talk, rest, and laugh; having dinner with loved ones; reading Scripture; and prayer.

Because God created the first celestial heavens to display his glory, when he makes the new celestial heavens, they will fulfill this mission even better. That means we'll have to be able to see the stars. If that requires darkness, as it does now, then it seems to me that even if the New Jerusalem is never dark, there will be places to go where there is darkness that highlights the bright beauty of God's heavenly creations.

New Jerusalem

What is the New Jerusalem?

> *Revelation 21:2* . . . I saw the holy city, the new
> Jerusalem, coming down from God out of heaven
> like a bride beautifully dressed for her husband.

The city at the center of the future Heaven, located on
the New Earth, is called the New Jerusalem. This will
be the capital city of the New Earth, which will be the
capital planet of the new universe.

> *Hebrews 12:22* . . . You have come to Mount Zion,
> to the city of the living God, the heavenly Jerusalem,
> and to countless thousands of angels in a joyful
> gathering.

> *Revelation 21:15-16, 19* . . . The angel who talked to
> me held in his hand a gold measuring stick to measure
> the city, its gates, and its wall. When he measured it, he
> found it was a square, as wide as it was long. In fact, its
> length and width and height were each 1,400 miles. . . .
> The wall of the city was built on foundation stones
> inlaid with twelve precious stones.

Fifteen times in Revelation 21 and 22 the place God and his people will live together is called a city. The repetition of the word and the detailed description of the architecture, walls, streets, and other features of the city strongly suggest that the term *city* isn't merely a figure of speech but a literal geographical location.

What will the great city be like?

> *Revelation 21:10-12 . . .* He took me in the Spirit
> to a great, high mountain, and he showed me the
> holy city, Jerusalem, descending out of heaven from
> God. It shone with the glory of God and sparkled
> like a precious stone—like jasper as clear as crystal.
> The city wall was broad and high, with twelve gates
> guarded by twelve angels.

Everyone knows what a city is—a place with buildings, streets, and residences occupied by people and subject to a common government. Cities have inhabitants, visitors, bustling activity, cultural events, and gatherings involving music, the arts, education, religion, entertainment, and athletics. If the capital city of the New Earth doesn't have these defining characteristics of a city, wouldn't it be misleading for Scripture to repeatedly call it a city?

> *Revelation 21:21 . . .* The twelve gates were made of
> pearls—each gate from a single pearl! And the main
> street was pure gold, as clear as glass.

The New Jerusalem will be a place of extravagant beauty and natural wonders. It will be a vast Eden, integrated with the best of human culture, under the reign of Christ. More wealth than has been accumulated in all human history will be spread freely across this immense city.

> *Hebrews 11:10* . . . Abraham was confidently looking forward to a city with eternal foundations, a city designed and built by God.

This city will have all the advantages we associate with earthly cities but none of the disadvantages. The city will be filled with natural wonders, magnificent architecture, thriving culture—but it will have no crime, pollution, sirens, traffic fatalities, garbage, or homelessness. It will truly be Heaven on Earth.

Oceans

Will there be oceans on the New Earth?

> *Revelation 21:1* . . . I saw a new heaven and a new
> earth, for the old heaven and the old earth had
> disappeared. And the sea was also gone.

One of the confusing—and to many people disap-
pointing—statements of Scripture is that on the New
Earth there will be no sea. When we read that, what
comes to mind is loss. We think it means there will be
no more warm, inviting waters; no more surfing, tide
pools, snorkeling and fun on the beach; and no more
wonderful sea creatures. That's bad news.

But when Scripture says the sea will be gone,
to the original readers it was gain, not loss. Why?
Because it meant there will be no more of the cold,
treacherous waters that separate nations, destroy
ships, and drown loved ones. There will be no more
creatures swallowing up seafarers and no more poi-
soned salt waters. That's good news. And a "sea" without salt water, without the great dangers and threat to

humanity, would no longer be a sea as we have always thought of it.

Even if Revelation 21:1 literally means there will be no more oceans, not even oceans restored to their original state, it still leaves the door open for large bodies of water. In fact, in a passage that seems clearly to speak of the New Earth, God tells Ezekiel that the great river of the redeemed city will make the sea into fresh water (Ezekiel 47:7-12).

Because most of God's animal creations reside in the oceans, even if they were no longer saltwater seas, it would be easy for him to make those creatures to live in fresh water if he so desires it.

> *Revelation 22:1-2* . . . The angel showed me a river with the water of life, clear as crystal, flowing from the throne of God and of the Lamb. It flowed down the center of the main street.

Scripture tells us a great river flows right through the capital city. How much more water will there be outside the city? Flowing rivers go somewhere. We would expect lakes, including very large ones. Some of the world's lakes are huge, sealike. The New Earth could have even larger lakes, especially if they have no oceans to flow into. Huge lakes could, in effect, be fresh-water oceans. We could end up living with all that was good about the oceans, with nothing that was bad about them.

Pets

Will our pets be restored on the New Earth?

> *Romans 8:18-23* . . . What we suffer now is nothing
> compared to the glory he will reveal to us later. For all
> creation is waiting eagerly for that future day when
> God will reveal who his children really are. Against
> its will, all creation was subjected to God's curse. But
> with eager hope, the creation looks forward to the day
> when it will join God's children in glorious freedom
> from death and decay. For we know that all creation
> has been groaning as in the pains of childbirth right
> up to the present time. And we believers also groan,
> even though we have the Holy Spirit within us as a
> foretaste of future glory.

I spoke earlier of the clear biblical promise of animals
living on the New Earth. But many people want to
know whether their pets might live again.

Why do so many people find such companionship,
solace, and joy in their pets? I believe it's because of
how God has made animals, and us. Animals aren't
nearly as valuable as people, but God is their Maker

and has touched many people's lives through them. We know animals will be on the New Earth, which is a redeemed and renewed old Earth, in which animals had a prominent role. Romans 8:19-23 sees animals as part of a suffering creation eagerly awaiting deliverance through humanity's resurrection. This seems to require that some animals who lived, suffered, and died on the old Earth must be made whole on the New Earth. Wouldn't some of those likely be our pets? Wouldn't it be just like God to take animals entrusted to our care in the old world and allow us to enjoy with them the wonders of the new world?

Physical Space

Will we live in a spatial Heaven?

> *Luke 24:39* . . . [Jesus said,] "Look at my hands. Look
> at my feet. You can see that it's really me. Touch me
> and make sure that I am not a ghost, because ghosts
> don't have bodies, as you see that I do."

The resurrected Christ walked on Earth; we will walk
on the New Earth. He occupied space; so will we. The
doctrine of resurrection is an emphatic statement that
we will forever occupy space. We'll be physical human
beings living in a physical universe.

> *Mark 13:27* . . . He will send out his angels to gather
> his chosen ones from all over the world—from the
> farthest ends of the earth and heaven.

As I indicated earlier, even the present Heaven appears
to occupy space. But certainly the new heavens and the
New Earth will. Resurrection doesn't eliminate God's
creations of space and time; it redeems them.

Possessions

Will there be private ownership in Heaven?

> *Matthew 6:20,* NIV . . . Store up for yourselves
> treasures in heaven.

> *Luke 16:12,* NIV . . . If you have not been trustworthy
> with someone else's property, who will give you
> property of your own?

> *2 Corinthians 5:10* . . . We must all stand before
> Christ to be judged. We will each receive whatever
> we deserve for the good or evil we have done in this
> earthly body.

> *Daniel 12:13* . . . At the end of the days, you will rise
> again to receive the inheritance set aside for you.

> *Colossians 3:24* . . . Remember that the Lord will
> give you an inheritance as your reward, and that
> the Master you are serving is Christ.

Jesus says that those who have properly stewarded
God's assets on Earth will be granted ownership of

assets in Heaven. He suggested that by parting with treasures now, we invest them in Heaven, where they'll be waiting for us when we arrive. This inheritance is given by the Father to the individual child in recognition of proven character and faithfulness.

> *Revelation 2:17* . . . To everyone who is victorious I will give some of the manna that has been hidden away in heaven. And I will give to each one a white stone, and on the stone will be engraved a new name that no one understands except the one who receives it.

What God gives you will be yours. Is this ownership wrong or selfish? No. Materialism, greed, envy, and selfishness are sins; ownership is not. Ownership is never wrong when God distributes to us possessions he wants us to own. The universe belongs to God, and he is free to give to us and others whatever he chooses. And, of course, we will find our greatest delight in sharing what's ours with others.

Will we miss things from the old Earth?

> *Isaiah 65:17* . . . Look! I am creating new heavens and
> a new earth, and no one will even think about the old
> ones anymore.

> *1 Peter 1:3–4* . . . All praise to God, the Father
> of our Lord Jesus Christ. It is by his great mercy
> that we have been born again, because God raised
> Jesus Christ from the dead. Now we live with great
> expectation, and we have a priceless inheritance—an
> inheritance that is kept in heaven for you, pure and
> undefiled, beyond the reach of change and decay.

Have you ever bought an economy ticket for a flight,
but because of overbooking or some other reason,
you were upgraded to first class? Did you regret the
upgrade? Did you spend your time wondering, *What
am I missing out on by not being in the back of the plane?*

The upgrade from the old Earth to the New Earth
will be vastly superior to that from economy to first
class. Gone will be sin, the Curse, death, and suffering.
In every way we will recognize that the New Earth is

better—in no sense could it ever be worse. If we would miss something from our old lives and the old Earth, it would be available to us on the New Earth. Why? Because we will experience all God intends for us. He fashions us to want precisely what he will give us, so what he gives us will be exactly what we want.

Privacy

Will we have privacy in Heaven?

> *Revelation 2:17* . . . I will give to each one a white
> stone, and on the stone will be engraved a new
> name that no one understands except the one
> who receives it.

A name known only to the recipient and God is private, indicating God will relate to us as individuals, not
just as one large group.

> *Luke 16:9,* NIV . . . I tell you, use worldly wealth to
> gain friends for yourselves, so that when it is gone,
> you will be welcomed into eternal dwellings.

> *John 14:2,* NIV . . . In my Father's house are many
> rooms. . . . I am going there to prepare a place
> for you.

The fact that people will have individual dwelling
places indicates privacy. So does Christ's statement
that God's house has many rooms. Rooms speak of

private dwellings within a larger dwelling. There is not just one public room in God's house, but many private places for his children to go.

Relationships

Will we desire relationships with anyone except God?

> *Genesis 2:18* . . . The LORD God said, "It is not good
> for the man to be alone. I will make a helper who is
> just right for him."

> *1 Thessalonians 2:17* . . . Dear brothers and sisters, after
> we were separated from you for a little while (though
> our hearts never left you), we tried very hard to come
> back because of our intense longing to see you again.

God has designed us for relationship not only with
himself but also with others of our kind. God planned
for Adam, and all mankind, to need human companionship. In other words, God made people to need and
desire others besides himself. Think of it—God was
with Adam in the Garden, yet God said that wasn't
good enough. God designed us to need each other.
What we gain from each other is more of God because
we're created in his image and are a conduit for his
self-revelation.

> *Matthew 22:37-39* . . . Jesus [said], "'You must love
> the LORD your God with all your heart, all your
> soul, and all your mind.' This is the first and greatest
> commandment. A second is equally important: 'Love
> your neighbor as yourself.'"

Jesus affirmed that the greatest commandment was to
love God, but that the second, inseparable from the
first, was to love our neighbor. He never considered
these commands incompatible. He saw the second
flowing directly from the first. One of the highest ways
we love God is by loving people.

> *1 Thessalonians 2:19-20* . . . What gives us hope and
> joy, and what will be our proud reward and crown as
> we stand before our Lord Jesus when he returns? It
> is you! Yes, you are our pride and joy.

Paul anticipates his ongoing relationship with the
Thessalonians as part of his heavenly reward. Isn't this
emphatic proof that it's appropriate for us to deeply
love people and look forward to being with them in
Heaven?

Some falsely assume that when we give attention to people it automatically distracts us from God. But even now, in a fallen world, people can turn my attention to God. Was Jesus distracted from God by spending time with people on Earth? Certainly not. In Heaven, no person will distract us from God. We will never experience any conflict between worshiping God himself and enjoying God's people. Our source of comfort isn't only that we'll be with the Lord in Heaven but also that we'll be with each other. We'll sit at feasts not only with God, but with his people. That is his design, and we should look forward to it.

Will we recognize each other in Heaven?

> *John 21:12* . . . "Come and have some breakfast!" Jesus
> said. None of the disciples dared to ask him, "Who
> are you?" They knew it was the Lord.

> *John 20:27* . . . [Jesus] said to Thomas, "Put your
> finger here, and look at my hands. Put your hand into
> the wound in my side. Don't be faithless any longer.
> Believe!"

> *1 Corinthians 15:6* . . . He was seen by more than
> 500 of his followers at one time, most of whom are
> still alive, though some have died.

Christ's disciples recognized him countless times after
his resurrection. The only two times when he was not
immediately recognized, by Mary and the disciples
on the Emmaus road, were the exceptions rather than
the rule.

> *1 Thessalonians 4:13-18* . . . Dear brothers and
> sisters, we want you to know what will happen to
> the believers who have died so you will not grieve

like people who have no hope. For since we believe that Jesus died and was raised to life again, we also believe that when Jesus returns, God will bring back with him the believers who have died. . . . For the Lord himself will come down from heaven with a commanding shout, with the voice of the archangel, and with the trumpet call of God. First, the believers who have died will rise from their graves. Then, together with them, we who are still alive and remain on the earth will be caught up in the clouds to meet the Lord in the air. Then we will be with the Lord forever. So encourage each other with these words.

Scripture gives no indication of a memory wipe causing us not to recognize family and friends. Paul anticipated being with the Thessalonians in Heaven, and it never occurred to him he wouldn't know them. In fact, if we wouldn't know our loved ones, the "encouragement" of an afterlife reunion would be no encouragement at all.

Will we regain lost relational opportunities?

> *Luke 6:21-23* . . . God blesses you who are hungry now, for you will be satisfied. God blesses you who weep now, for in due time you will laugh. What blessings await you when people hate you and exclude you and mock you and curse you as evil because you follow the Son of Man. When that happens, be happy! Yes, leap for joy! For a great reward awaits you in heaven.

> *2 Peter 3:13* . . . We are looking forward to the new heavens and new earth he has promised, a world filled with God's righteousness.

Relationships among God's people will resume in ways even better than what we've known here. Heaven offers more than comfort; it offers compensation. In the same way that the hungry will fill up in Heaven and those who weep will laugh, will those who suffer tragedy experience a compensating victory? For those who know God, he's a God who redeems lost opportunities—especially those lost through our faithful service.

Once the Curse is lifted and death is forever reversed, we may live out many of the "could have beens" taken from us on the old Earth. I think it's likely that two friends who always dreamed of going to a special place, but never managed to, will be able to go to that very place on the New Earth.

Remembering the Old Earth

What will we remember about Earth?

> *Isaiah 65:16*, NIV . . . The past troubles will be
> forgotten and hidden from my eyes.

> *Jeremiah 31:34* . . . I will never again remember
> their sins.

God chooses not to bring up our past sins or hold them against us. In eternity, past sins and sorrows won't preoccupy God or us. We'll be capable of choosing not to recall or dwell on anything about our pasts that would diminish Heaven's eternal joy.

> *Revelation 6:9-10* . . . I saw under the altar the souls
> of all who had been martyred for the word of God
> and for being faithful in their testimony. They
> shouted to the Lord and said, "O Sovereign Lord,
> holy and true, how long before you judge the people
> who belong to this world and avenge our blood for
> what they have done to us?"

The martyrs in the present Heaven remember what happened on Earth, including that they endured great suffering. This memory wasn't incompatible with their experience of Heaven.

> *Luke 16:24-25* . . . [Jesus said,] "The rich man shouted, 'Father Abraham, have some pity! Send Lazarus over here to dip the tip of his finger in water and cool my tongue. I am in anguish in these flames.' But Abraham said to him, 'Son, remember that during your lifetime you had everything you wanted, and Lazarus had nothing. So now he is here being comforted, and you are in anguish.'"

Jesus promised that in Heaven, those who endured bad things on Earth would be comforted. The comfort implies memory of what happened. If we had no memory of the bad things, why would we need comfort? How would we feel it?

> *John 20:27* . . . [Jesus] said to Thomas, "Put your finger here, and look at my hands. Put your hand into the wound in my side. Don't be faithless any longer. Believe!"

Christ's resurrection body has nail-scarred hands and feet. Seeing those scars in Heaven will always remind us that our sins nailed Jesus to the cross. Heaven's happiness won't be dependent on our ignorance of what happened on Earth. Rather, it will be enhanced by our informed appreciation of God's glorious grace and justice as we grasp what really happened here. Our minds will be clearer in Heaven, not foggier. Memory is basic to personality. The biblical principle of continuity from this life to the next requires not that we will dwell on our past lives, but that we will remember them.

Revelation 21:12 . . . The city wall was broad and high, with twelve gates guarded by twelve angels. And the names of the twelve tribes of Israel were written on the gates.

Revelation 21:14 . . . The wall of the city had twelve foundation stones, and on them were written the names of the twelve apostles of the Lamb.

The New Earth will include memorials to the twelve tribes and the apostles. This indicates continuity and memory of history. If we're aware of others' pasts on the old Earth, surely we'll be aware of our own.

Will we miss the old Earth?

> *Revelation 22:1-2* . . . A river with the water of life . . .
> flowed down the center of the main street. On each
> side of the river grew a tree of life, bearing twelve
> crops of fruit, with a fresh crop each month. The
> leaves were used for medicine to heal the nations.

The New Earth will be a place of healing. Whenever
Jesus healed people, the act spoke of wholeness and
health, the original perfection of Adam and Eve, and
the coming perfection of resurrected bodies and spirits.
Everything changes when we grasp that all we love
about the old Earth will be ours on the New Earth—
either in the same form or in another. Once we understand this, we won't regret leaving all the wonders of
the world we've seen or mourn not having seen its
countless other wonders. Why? *Because we will yet be
able to see them.* God is no more done with the earth
than he's done with us.

Resurrection

Why is the resurrection of our bodies so important to our view of Heaven?

> *1 Corinthians 15:17-19* . . . If Christ has not been raised, then your faith is useless and you are still guilty of your sins. . . . And if our hope in Christ is only for this life, we are more to be pitied than anyone in the world.

> *Philippians 3:20-21* . . . We are citizens of heaven, where the Lord Jesus Christ lives. And we are eagerly waiting for him to return as our Savior. He will take our weak mortal bodies and change them into glorious bodies like his own, using the same power with which he will bring everything under his control.

> *1 Corinthians 15:49* . . . Just as we are now like the earthly man, we will someday be like the heavenly man.

The physical resurrection of Jesus Christ is the cornerstone of redemption, both for mankind and for the earth. Indeed, without Christ's resurrection and what it means—an eternal future for fully restored human beings dwelling on a fully restored earth—there is no Christianity. It is our bodily resurrection that will allow us to return to an earthly life, this time freed from sin and the Curse.

This, then, is the most basic truth about our resurrected bodies: They are the same bodies God created for us, but they will be raised to greater perfection than we've ever known. God will not scrap his original creation and start over. Instead, he will take his fallen, corrupted children and restore, refresh, and renew us to our original design. If *resurrection* had meant the creation of a new body, Christ's original body would have remained in the tomb.

When we receive our resurrected bodies, we'll no doubt have some welcome surprises, maybe even some new features (though no glitches). But we'll certainly recognize our new bodies as being distinctly *ours*. God has given us these working prototypes of our current bodies to guide our understanding about what our new bodies will be like on the New Earth.

Genesis 2:7 . . . The Lᴏʀᴅ God formed the man from the dust of the ground. He breathed the breath of life into the man's nostrils, and the man became a living person.

Job 19:26 . . . And after my body has decayed, yet in my body I will see God!

Our physical bodies are an essential aspect of who we are, not just shells for our spirits to inhabit. Adam was not a living human being until he had both material (physical) and immaterial (spiritual) components. Thus, the essence of humanity is not just spirit, but *spirit joined with body*. Your body does not merely house the real you—it is as much a part of who you are as your spirit is. That's why the bodily resurrection of the dead is so vital. And that's why Job rejoiced that *in his body* he would see God.

Rest

Will we rest in Heaven?

Genesis 2:2 . . . On the seventh day God had finished his work of creation, so he rested from all his work.

Exodus 20:9-11 . . . You have six days each week for your ordinary work, but the seventh day is a Sabbath day of rest dedicated to the LORD your God. On that day no one in your household may do any work. This includes you, your sons and daughters, your male and female servants, your livestock, and any foreigners living among you. For in six days the LORD made the heavens, the earth, the sea, and everything in them; but on the seventh day he rested. That is why the LORD blessed the Sabbath day and set it apart as holy.

Leviticus 25:4-5 . . . During the seventh year the land must have a Sabbath year of complete rest. It is the LORD's Sabbath. Do not plant your fields or prune your vineyards during that year. And don't store away the crops that grow on their own or gather the grapes from your unpruned vines. The land must have a year of complete rest.

When God created the world, he rested on the seventh day. That's the basis for the biblical Sabbath, when all people and even the animals rested. God set aside days and weeks of rest, and he even rested the earth itself every seventh year. This is the rest we can anticipate on the New Earth—times of joyful praise and relaxed fellowship. Work will be refreshing on the New Earth, yet regular rest will be built into our lives.

Hebrews 4:3 . . . Only we who believe can enter his rest. As for the others, God said, "In my anger I took an oath: 'They will never enter my place of rest,'" even though this rest has been ready since he made the world.

Hebrews 4:9 . . . There is a special rest still waiting for the people of God.

Revelation 14:13 . . . I heard a voice from heaven saying, "Write this down: Blessed are those who die in the Lord from now on. Yes, says the Spirit, they are blessed indeed, for they will rest from their hard work; for their good deeds follow them!"

What feels better than putting your head on the pillow after a hard day's work? How about what it will feel like after a hard life's work? God rested on the seventh day, before sin entered the world. God didn't need to rest himself, but he did, showing us that even if we think we don't need rest, it's a part of his design for life. Regular rest will be woven into our lives in the new universe.

Rewards

How should the promise of compensation in Heaven affect us now?

> *Luke 14:14* . . . At the resurrection of the righteous, God will reward you for inviting those who could not repay you.

> *Matthew 6:19-20* . . . Don't store up treasures here on earth, where moths eat them and rust destroys them, and where thieves break in and steal. Store your treasures in heaven, where moths and rust cannot destroy, and thieves do not break in and steal.

The lack of an eternal perspective sets us up not only for discouragement but sin. We feel desperate, tempted to take shortcuts to get what we want. Or we live in regret, greed, and envy. But if we understand that we'll actually live in a new heavens and New Earth, a new universe full of new opportunities, then we can forgo certain pleasures and experiences now, knowing we can enjoy them later. So, it's not only virtuous for us to make sacrifices for the needy now; it's also wise. The treasures we lay up in Heaven will be ours to enjoy and share forever.

Sex

Will there be sex?

> *Matthew 22:30* . . . When the dead rise, they will
> neither marry nor be given in marriage. In this
> respect they will be like the angels in heaven.

> *Hosea 2:16, 19-20* . . . "When that day comes," says
> the LORD, "you will call me 'my husband' instead
> of 'my master.' . . . I will make you my wife forever,
> showing you righteousness and justice, unfailing love
> and compassion. I will be faithful to you and make
> you mine, and you will finally know me as the LORD."

> *Psalm 103:11* . . . His unfailing love . . . is as great as
> the height of the heavens above the earth.

Sexual relations existed before the Fall and were *not*
the product of sin and the Curse; they were God's
original and perfect design. Because the lifting of the
Curse will normally restore what God originally made,
we would expect sex to be part of that. However, as
we've seen, Christ appears to have made it clear that

people in Heaven wouldn't be married to each other (though some claim it only means there won't be new marriages, while old marriages will continue). Because sex was designed to be part of a marriage relationship, marriage and sex logically belong together. Since we're told that humans won't be married to each other, and sex is intended for marriage, then logically, it seems to me, it means we won't be engaging in sex.

There's a different sort of continuity between earthly marriage and the marriage of Christ to his church, so there may also be some way in which the intimacy and pleasure we now know as sex will be fulfilled in some higher form we don't now understand. If we won't have sex and if in Heaven there's no frustration of desire, then obviously we won't desire sex. What we will desire and always enjoy is the best part of sex—what sex was always pointing to—deep and transcendent relational intimacy.

Sin

Can we know we won't sin or be tempted in Heaven?

> *Matthew 13:41* . . . The Son of Man will send his
> angels, and they will remove from his Kingdom
> everything that causes sin and all who do evil.

> *Romans 6:23* . . . The wages of sin is death, but the
> free gift of God is eternal life through Christ Jesus
> our Lord.

> *Revelation 21:4* . . . There will be no more death
> or sorrow or crying or pain. All these things are
> gone forever.

> *Hebrews 10:10* . . . God's will was for us to be made
> holy by the sacrifice of the body of Jesus Christ, once
> for all time.

God will send his angels to remove not only sin, but
everything that *causes* sin. Sin will be a thing of the
past. Because the wages of sin is death, if we cannot die, then it presupposes we cannot sin. Scripture

emphasizes that Christ died *once* to deal with sin and will never again need to die. We won't sin in Heaven for the same reason God doesn't: He cannot sin. Our eternal inability to sin has been purchased by Christ's blood. Our Savior purchased our perfection *for all time*.

Romans 6:7 . . . When we died with Christ we were set free from the power of sin.

Christ will not allow us to be vulnerable to the very thing he died to deliver us from. Because our righteousness is rooted in Christ, who is eternally righteous, we can never lose it. Because our hearts will be pure and we'll see people as they truly are, every relationship in Heaven will be pure. We'll all be faithful to the love of our lives: King Jesus. We couldn't do anything behind his back even if we wanted to. But we'll never want to. We'll see sin as God does. It will be stripped of its illusions and will be utterly and eternally unappealing.

Sleep

Will we sleep in Heaven?

> *Leviticus 26:6* . . . I will give you peace in the land, and
> you will be able to sleep with no cause for fear.

> *Psalm 4:8* . . . In peace I will lie down and sleep, for
> you alone, O LORD, will keep me safe.

> *Ezekiel 34:25-26* . . . I will make a covenant of peace
> with my people and drive away the dangerous animals
> from the land. Then they will be able to camp safely
> in the wildest places and sleep in the woods without
> fear. I will bless my people and their homes around
> my holy hill.

Sleep is one of life's great pleasures. It's part of God's
perfect plan for humans in bodies living on the earth.
To need sleep is not to be fallen, but to be finite. There's
no reason to believe that Adam and Eve, before sin
entered the world, didn't sleep. Troubled sleep and
sleeplessness are products of sin and the Curse, but
sleep itself is God's gift. It's a matter of God's design

for the rhythm of life. On the New Earth, we may need it and enjoy it. If we will eat, walk, serve, work, laugh, and play, why would we not sleep? We know we'll rest and be refreshed in Heaven. What's more restful and refreshing than a good sleep?

Space and the Universe

What will the new celestial heavens be like?

> *Isaiah 65:17* . . . Look! I am creating new heavens and
> a new earth.

> *Revelation 21:1-3* . . . I saw a new heaven and a
> new earth, for the old heaven and the old earth
> had disappeared. And the sea was also gone. And
> I saw the holy city, the new Jerusalem, coming
> down from God out of heaven like a bride
> beautifully dressed for her husband. I heard a loud
> shout from the throne, saying, "Look, God's home
> is now among his people! He will live with them,
> and they will be his people. God himself will be
> with them."

The Bible's final two chapters make clear that every
aspect of the new creation will be greater than the old.
The new heavens will surely be superior to the old
heavens, which themselves are filled with untold billions of stars and likely trillions of planets.

Psalm 148:3-6 . . . Praise him, sun and moon! Praise him, all you twinkling stars! Praise him, skies above! Praise him, vapors high above the clouds! Let every created thing give praise to the LORD, for he issued his command, and they came into being. He set them in place forever and ever. His decree will never be revoked.

While some passages suggest that the universe will wear out and the stars will be destroyed, others indicate that the stars will exist forever. Is this a contradiction? No. We too will be destroyed by death, yet we will last forever. The earth will be destroyed by God's judgment, yet it will last forever. In exactly the same way, the stars will be destroyed, yet they will last forever. Based on the redemptive work of Christ, God will resurrect them, to his eternal glory.

Revelation 2:28 . . . They will have the same authority I received from my Father, and I will also give them the morning star!

The morning star is a celestial object—the planet Venus. Although most people consider Jesus' statement to be figurative, it could suggest that God might entrust to his children planets or stars (with their respective planetary systems) in the new heavens. Because the whole universe fell under mankind's sin, we can conclude that the whole universe was intended to be under mankind's dominion. If so, then the entire new universe will be ours to explore, inhabit, and rule—to God's glory. Venus as it is now is a hellish planet. A redeemed Venus might be startlingly beautiful.

What has God made in the heights of distant galaxies, never seen by human eyes? One day we'll behold those wonders, soaking them in with openmouthed awe. And if that won't be enough, we may see wonders God held back in his first creation, wonders that will cause us to marvel and drop to our knees in worship when we behold them in the new creation.

Will we be able to travel through space and explore it?

Isaiah 65:17 . . . Look! I am creating new heavens and
a new earth.

2 Peter 3:13 . . . We are looking forward to the new
heavens and new earth he has promised, a world filled
with God's righteousness.

God promises to make not only a New Earth but also
"new heavens." The Greek and Hebrew words translated "heavens" include the stars and planets and what
we call outer space. Because God will resurrect the old
Earth and the old Jerusalem, transforming both into
the new, shouldn't we understand "new heavens" as an
expression of his intention to resurrect galaxies, nebulae, stars, planets, and moons in a form as close to their
original form as the earth will be to its original form
and we will be to ours?

Psalm 19:1, NIV . . . The heavens declare the
glory of God; the skies proclaim the work of
his hands.

The stars of the heavens declare God's glory, yet how vast and different they are. God made countless billions of galaxies containing perhaps trillions of nebulae, planets, and moons. Not many in human history have seen more than a few thousand stars, and then only as dots in the sky. If the heavens declare God's glory now, and if we will spend eternity proclaiming God's glory, don't you think exploring the new heavens, and exercising dominion over them, will likely be part of God's plan? Many of us have taken pleasure traveling on this earth. What might it be like to travel both the New Earth and the new universe?

Will the New Earth have a sun and moon?

> *Revelation 21:23* . . . The city has no need of sun or moon, for the glory of God illuminates the city, and the Lamb is its light.

> *Revelation 22:5* . . . There will be no night there—no need for lamps or sun—for the Lord God will shine on them. And they will reign forever and ever.

> *Isaiah 60:19-21* . . . No longer will you need the sun to shine by day, nor the moon to give its light by night, for the Lord your God will be your everlasting light, and your God will be your glory. Your sun will never set; your moon will not go down. For the Lord will be your everlasting light. Your days of mourning will come to an end. All your people will be righteous. They will possess their land forever, for I will plant them there with my own hands in order to bring myself glory.

Notice that not one of these verses actually says there will be no more sun or moon. They all say that the New Jerusalem will not *need* their light, for sun and moon will be outshone by God's glory. The third passage says that at the time when God's people will possess the land forever, the sun won't set and the moon won't wane, yet neither will dominate the sky because of God's brighter light. The emphasis isn't on the *elimination* of sun and moon, but on their being *overshadowed* by the greater light of God. The sun is local and limited, easily obscured by clouds. God's light is universal, all pervading; nothing can obstruct it.

Sports

Will there be sports on the New Earth?

> *1 Corinthians 9:24* . . . Don't you realize that in a race everyone runs, but only one person gets the prize? So run to win!

> *2 Timothy 2:5* . . . Athletes cannot win the prize unless they follow the rules.

Scripture compares the Christian life to athletic competitions. Just as we can look forward to cultural endeavors such as art, drama, and music on the New Earth, we can assume that we'll also enjoy sports there. Given the principle of redemptive continuity, we should expect the New Earth to be characterized by familiar and earthly things. If the eternal Heaven were a disembodied state, obviously there would be no sports. But on a physical Earth with physical human beings, we should expect sports to be part of life and culture.

Remember, to be earthly is not to be "worldly," in the sin-corrupted sense, because God is the designer and creator of the earth. Because sports aren't inherently sinful, we have every reason to believe that the same activities, games, skills, and interests we enjoy here will be available on the New Earth, with many new ones we've never imagined.

Technology

Will technology be found on the New Earth, or will we return to the pristine environment of the original Garden of Eden?

> *Revelation 21:2, 10-11, 18, 21* . . . I saw the holy city, the new Jerusalem, coming down from God out of heaven like a bride beautifully dressed for her husband. . . . So he took me in the Spirit to a great, high mountain, and he showed me the holy city, Jerusalem, descending out of heaven from God. It shone with the glory of God and sparkled like a precious stone—like jasper as clear as crystal. . . . The wall was made of jasper, and the city was pure gold, as clear as glass. . . . The twelve gates were made of pearls—each gate from a single pearl! And the main street was pure gold, as clear as glass.

Some people expect the New Earth to be a return to Eden as it was, without technology or the accomplishments of civilization. But that doesn't fit the biblical picture of the great city, the New Jerusalem. Nor is it logical. Would we expect on the New Earth an unin-vention of the wheel? Or an eventual reinvention of it? There was direct continuity from the pre-Fall world to the post-Fall world. Similarly, there will be direct continuity between the dying old Earth and the resur-rected New Earth.

As Albert Wolters writes in his book *Creation Regained*, "By analogy, salvation in Jesus Christ, con-ceived in the broad creational sense, means a restora-tion of culture and society in their present stage of development. Life in the new creation will not be a repristination of all things—a going back to the way things were at the beginning. Rather, life in the new creation will be a restoration of all things—involving removal of every sinful impurity and the retaining of all that is holy and good."

Will there be new inventions? Refinements of old inventions?

> *Romans 11:29*, NIV . . . God's gifts and his call are irrevocable.

Why not? We'll live in resurrected bodies on a resurrected Earth. The God who gave people creativity surely won't take it back, will he? The gifts and calling of God are irrevocable. When God gave Eden to Adam and Eve, he expected them to develop it. He'll give us the New Earth and expect the same of us. But this time we'll succeed! This time no human accomplishment, no cultural masterpiece, no technological achievement will be marred by sin and death. All will fully serve God's purposes and bring him glory. Technology is a God-given aspect of human capability that enables us to fulfill his command to exercise dominion.

Time

Will we experience time in Heaven?

> *Revelation 6:10-11*, NIV . . . [The martyrs] called
> out in a loud voice, "How long, Sovereign Lord,
> holy and true, until you judge the inhabitants of the
> earth and avenge our blood?" Then each of them was
> given a white robe, and they were told to wait a little
> longer, until the number of their fellow servants and
> brothers who were to be killed as they had been was
> completed.

Martyrs in Heaven are told to "wait a little longer"
when they ask "how long" before Christ will judge
the inhabitants of the earth and avenge the martyrs'
blood. Those in Heaven couldn't ask "how long" or be
told "wait a little longer" unless time actually passes in
Heaven.

> *Revelation 22:2*, NIV . . . On each side of the river
> stood the tree of life, bearing twelve crops of fruit,
> yielding its fruit every month.

The tree of life on the New Earth will be "yielding its fruit every month." There will clearly be days and months on the New Earth.

> *Revelation 8:1* . . . When the Lamb broke the seventh seal on the scroll, there was silence throughout heaven for about half an hour.

> *Revelation 4:10* . . . The twenty-four elders fall down and worship the one sitting on the throne (the one who lives forever and ever). And they lay their crowns before the throne.

The book of Revelation shows the present Heaven's inhabitants operating within time—after the seal was broken, the silence is said to have lasted "about half an hour." The descriptions include successive actions, such as falling down at God's throne and laying crowns before him. There's a sequence of events; things occur one after another, not all at once. Will we still live in chronological sequence, where one word, step, or event follows the previous and is followed by the next? Though it goes against many people's assumptions about Heaven, the Bible's clear answer is yes.

1 Corinthians 15:26 . . . The last enemy to be destroyed is death.

People imagine time is an enemy because the clock seems to move so slowly when we're having a root canal and so quickly when we're on vacation. But time isn't the problem, the Curse is. Time isn't the enemy, death is. Time predated sin and the Curse. When the Curse is lifted, time will remain, having been redeemed. The passing of time will no longer threaten us. It will bring new adventures without a sense of loss for what must end. We'll live *with* time, no longer *under* its pressure.

Time Travel

Will we travel in time?

> *Daniel 9:23* . . . The moment you began praying, a
> command was given. And now I am here to tell you
> what it was, for you are very precious to God.

Usually, we're not able to see God's immediate responses to our prayers. But in Heaven, God may permit us to see what happened in the spiritual realm when he answered our prayers. In the Old Testament, an angel comes to the prophet Daniel and tells him what happened as a result of his prayers.

> *Ephesians 2:7* . . . God can point to us in all future
> ages as examples of the incredible wealth of his grace
> and kindness toward us, as shown in all he has done
> for us who are united with Christ Jesus.

Even though I believe Scripture shows we'll live in time, God is certainly capable of bending time and opening doors in time's fabric for us. Because God is not limited by time, he may choose to show us past events as if they were presently happening. We may be able to study history from a front-row seat. Can you imagine being there as Jesus preaches the Sermon on the Mount? Want to see the crossing of the Red Sea? Want to be there when Daniel's three friends emerge from the fiery furnace? Perhaps we'll have opportunity to see the lives of our spiritual and physical ancestors lived out on Earth.

One reason God might do this is to show us his providence, grace, and goodness in our lives and the lives of others. Wouldn't that bring God glory? Wouldn't it cause us to praise and exalt him for his sovereign grace? Couldn't this fit his revealed purpose to point to us as "examples of the incredible wealth of his grace and kindness toward us"?

Tree of Life

What is the tree of life?

> *Genesis 2:8-9; 3:22-23* . . . The Lord God planted a
> garden in Eden in the east, and there he placed the
> man he had made. The Lord God made all sorts
> of trees grow up from the ground. . . . In the middle
> of the garden he placed the tree of life and the tree of
> the knowledge of good and evil. . . . Then the Lord
> God said, "Look, the human beings have become like
> us, knowing both good and evil. What if they reach
> out, take fruit from the tree of life, and eat it? Then
> they will live forever!" So the Lord God banished
> them from the Garden of Eden.

> *Revelation 2:7* . . . To everyone who is victorious
> I will give fruit from the tree of life in the paradise
> of God.

> *Revelation 21:2* . . . I saw the holy city, the new
> Jerusalem, coming down from God out of
> heaven like a bride beautifully dressed for her
> husband.

The tree of life is mentioned in Genesis 2 and 3, in Eden, and again in Revelation. These instances seem to refer to Eden's literal tree of life. Adam and Eve were designed to live forever, but to do so they likely needed to eat from the tree of life. Once they sinned, they were banned from the Garden, separated from the tree, and subject to physical death, just as they had experienced spiritual death. Since Eden, death has reigned throughout history. But on the New Earth, our access to the tree of life will be forever restored.

We're told the tree of life is presently in Paradise, the intermediate Heaven (Revelation 2:7). The New Jerusalem itself, also in the present Heaven, will be brought down, tree of life and all, and placed on the New Earth. Just as the tree was apparently relocated from Eden to the present Heaven, it will be relocated again to the New Earth. The presence of this specific tree indicates that the essence of Eden will be restored to the earth. The massive increase in its size, growing on both banks of a river, suggests the tree of life will become more of a forest of life, in keeping with the growth of humanity's population and dominion over the earth.

> *Revelation 22:2* . . . [The river] flowed down the center of the main street. On each side of the river grew a tree of life, bearing twelve crops of fruit, with a fresh crop each month. The leaves were used for medicine to heal the nations.

In the New Earth, we will freely eat the fruit of the same tree that nourished Adam and Eve. Apparently our physical life and health, even our healing, will come not from our intrinsic immortal nature but from regularly partaking of God's gracious provision in the fruit and leaves of the tree of life. We will never suffer and die because we will never be separated from our source of eternal wellness.

Unfulfilled Dreams

Will unfulfilled dreams be realized in Heaven?

> *Luke 6:20-23* . . . Jesus turned to his disciples
> and said, "God blesses you who are poor, for the
> Kingdom of God is yours. God blesses you who are
> hungry now, for you will be satisfied. God blesses
> you who weep now, for in due time you will laugh.
> What blessings await you when people hate you
> and exclude you and mock you and curse you as
> evil because you follow the Son of Man. When
> that happens, be happy! Yes, leap for joy! For a
> great reward awaits you in heaven."

Jesus tells the hungry they'll be satisfied. Those whose eyes are swollen with tears will laugh. Those persecuted should leap for joy now. Why? Because of their great reward in Heaven later. This planet is the setting for God's ultimate comfort, for his reversal of life's injustices and tragedies. God promises to make up for the heartbreaks of this life. All the blessings Jesus promised will be ours in the place where we will live—the New Earth.

Romans 8:18 . . . What we suffer now is nothing
compared to the glory he will reveal to us later.

Are you living with the disappointment of unfulfilled
dreams? In Heaven you'll find their fulfillment. Did
poverty, poor health, war, or lack of time prevent you
from pursuing an adventure or dream? Did you never
get to finish building that boat or painting that picture
or writing that book—or reading that pile of books?
Good news. On the New Earth you may well have
a second chance, or an eternity of renewed opportunities, to do what you dreamed of doing—and far
more besides.

Weather

Will there be seasons and varying weather on the New Earth?

> *Job 37:3-6* . . . [God's] lightning flashes in every direction. Then comes the roaring of the thunder— the tremendous voice of his majesty. He does not restrain it when he speaks. God's voice is glorious in the thunder. We can't even imagine the greatness of his power. He directs the snow to fall on the earth and tells the rain to pour down.

Some people have never thought about Heaven's weather because they don't think of Heaven as a real place, certainly not an earthly one. Or they assume the New Earth will have bright sunshine, no clouds, no rain . . . forever. Lightning, thunder, rain, and snow all declare God's greatness. Is there any reason to conclude such things will not be a part of the New Earth?

Of course, no one will die or be hurt by such weather. No one will perish in a flood or be killed by lightning, just as no one will drown in the river of life. Nature, including variations in climate, will be a source of joy and pleasure, not destruction. If we stand amazed now at the wonders of God's great creation, we'll be far more amazed at the greater wonders of that greater creation.

> *Ezekiel 34:26-27* . . . I will bless my people and their homes around my holy hill. And in the proper season I will send the showers they need. There will be showers of blessing. The orchards and fields of my people will yield bumper crops.

Is rain a bad thing? No. It's good. We'll see trees bearing fruit on the New Earth. Will they be rained on? Presumably. Will rain turn to snow in higher elevations? Why not? If there's snow, will people play in it, throw snowballs, and sled down hillsides? Why wouldn't they? Just as resurrected people will still have eyes, ears, and feet, resurrected Earth will presumably have rain, snow, and wind.

Work

Will we work on the New Earth?

> *Genesis 2:15*, NIV . . . The LORD God took the man
> and put him in the Garden of Eden to work it and
> take care of it.

> *Revelation 22:3*, NIV . . . No longer will there be any
> curse. The throne of God and of the Lamb will be
> in the city, and his servants will serve him.

> *Amos 9:13-14* . . . "The time will come," says the
> LORD, "when the grain and grapes will grow faster
> than they can be harvested. Then the terraced
> vineyards on the hills of Israel will drip with sweet
> wine! I will bring my exiled people of Israel back
> from distant lands, and they will rebuild their
> ruined cities and live in them again. They will plant
> vineyards and gardens; they will eat their crops and
> drink their wine."

Work wasn't part of the Curse. The Curse, rather, made
work menial, tedious, and frustrating (Genesis 3:17-19).

Because work began before sin and the Curse, and because God, who is without sin, is a worker, we should assume human beings will work on the New Earth. We'll have satisfying and enriching work that we can't wait to get back to, work that'll never be drudgery.

> *Colossians 3:23* . . . Work willingly at whatever you do, as though you were working for the Lord rather than for people.

> *Matthew 25:23,* NKJV . . . Well done, good and faithful servant; you have been faithful over a few things, I will make you ruler over many things. Enter into the joy of your lord.

How will we glorify God for eternity? By doing everything he tells us to do. What did God first tell mankind to do? Fill the earth and exercise dominion over it. What will we do for eternity to glorify God? We'll exercise dominion over the earth, demonstrating God's creativity and ingenuity as his image bearers, producing Christ-exalting culture.

John 5:17 . . . Jesus [said], "My Father is always working, and so am I."

John 4:34 . . . Jesus explained: "My nourishment comes from doing the will of God, who sent me, and from finishing his work."

God is the primary worker, and as his image bearers, we're made to work. Jesus found great satisfaction in his work. We create, accomplish, set goals, and fulfill them—to God's glory. Our work will be joyful and fulfilling, giving glory to God.

Will our work be interesting and engaging?

> *Ephesians 2:10* . . . We are God's masterpiece. He
> has created us anew in Christ Jesus, so we can do
> the good things he planned for us long ago.

> *Luke 19:17-19* . . . "Well done!" the king exclaimed.
> "You are a good servant. You have been faithful with
> the little I entrusted to you, so you will be governor of
> ten cities as your reward." The next servant reported,
> "Master, I invested your money and made five times
> the original amount." "Well done!" the king said.
> "You will be governor over five cities."

The God who created us to do good works will not
cancel this purpose when he resurrects us to inhabit
the new universe. The Bible's picture of resurrected
people at work in a vibrant society on a resurrected
Earth couldn't be more compelling: We're going to
help God run the universe.

Even under the Curse, we catch glimpses of how
work can be enriching, how it can build relationships,
and how it can help us to improve. Work stretches

us in ways that make us smarter, wiser, and more fulfilled. Work in Heaven won't be frustrating or fruitless; instead, it will involve lasting accomplishment, unhindered by decay and fatigue, enhanced by unlimited resources. Our best workdays on the present Earth—those days when everything turns out better than we planned, when we get everything done on time, and when everyone on the team pulls together and enjoys one another—are just a small foretaste of the joy our work will bring us on the New Earth.

Will our life's work continue in Heaven?

> *Revelation 14:13* . . . I heard a voice from heaven saying, "Write this down: Blessed are those who die in the Lord from now on. Yes, says the Spirit, they are blessed indeed, for they will rest from their hard work; for their good deeds follow them!"

Because there will be continuity from the old Earth to the new, it's possible we'll continue some of the work we started on the old Earth. We'll pursue some of the same things we were doing, or dreamed of doing, before our deaths. Of course, some people's jobs won't exist on the New Earth, among them dentists, police officers, funeral directors, and insurance salespeople. What are now their interests or hobbies may become their main vocations. Others might continue working as they do now, as gardeners, engineers, builders, artists, animal trainers, musicians, scientists, craftspeople, or hundreds of other vocations. A significant difference will be that they'll work without the hindrances of toil, pain, corruption, sin, and exhaustion. It will be the best we have experienced in our most fulfilling work, without any of the worst.

Does God value craftsmanship?

> *Exodus 31:1-5* . . . The LORD said to Moses, "Look,
> I have specifically chosen Bezalel son of Uri,
> grandson of Hur, of the tribe of Judah. I have filled
> him with the Spirit of God, giving him great wisdom,
> ability, and expertise in all kinds of crafts. He is a
> master craftsman, expert in working with gold, silver,
> and bronze. He is skilled in engraving and mounting
> gemstones and in carving wood. He is a master at
> every craft!"

The first person Scripture describes as filled with the Spirit of God wasn't a prophet or priest; he was a craftsman. God gifted and called Bezalel to be a skilled laborer, a master craftsman, a God-glorifying artist. The gifting and calling were from God. God is a maker. He'll never cease being a maker. God made us, his image bearers, to be makers. We'll never cease to be makers. When we die, we won't leave behind our creativity but only what hinders our ability to honor God through what we create.

Exodus 25:10-11; 26:1 . . . [The Lord said to
Moses,] "Have the people make an Ark of acacia
wood—a sacred chest 45 inches long, 27 inches
wide, and 27 inches high. Overlay it inside and
outside with pure gold, and run a molding of gold all
around it. . . . Make the Tabernacle from ten curtains
of finely woven linen. Decorate the curtains with
blue, purple, and scarlet thread and with skillfully
embroidered cherubim."

The Master Designer goes into great detail in his
instructions for building the Tabernacle: the veil
and curtain, the Ark of the Covenant, the table, the
lampstand, the altar of burnt offerings, the courtyard,
the incense altar, the washbasin, the priest's clothing
(Exodus 25–28). The design, precision, and beauty of
these things tell us about God, ourselves, and the culture on the New Earth.

Will there be trade and business?

> *Colossians 3:23-24* ... Work willingly at whatever you
> do, as though you were working for the Lord rather
> than for people. Remember that the Lord will give
> you an inheritance as your reward, and that the
> Master you are serving is Christ.

I believe we will see trade and business, although not
for all the same reasons we engage in them now. If we
dismiss the likelihood of business and commerce on
the New Earth, we send the wrong message: that business and commerce are part of the Curse, inherently
unspiritual or unimportant to God. Business is not the
result of sin but of human interdependence, creativity,
and variety. There's much more to business and trade
than putting food on the table or repairing the roof,
though those are good reasons. Whether you work in
a bookstore, bakery, or school, don't you experience joy
in using your knowledge, skills, services, and products
to help and please others? Sure, it's good and often
necessary to earn money, too, but that isn't the ultimate
source of joy.

PART IV

Can You Know You're Going to Heaven?

Can you know you're going to Heaven?

1 John 5:13 . . . I have written this to you who believe in the name of the Son of God, so that you may know you have eternal life.

1 Corinthians 15:42 . . . It is the same way with the resurrection of the dead. Our earthly bodies are planted in the ground when we die, but they will be raised to live forever.

Can we really know in advance where we're going when we die? The apostle John, the same one who wrote about the new heavens and New Earth, said in one of his letters we *can* know for sure that we have eternal life. We can know for sure that we will go to Heaven when we die.

John 3:16 . . . This is how God loved the world: He gave his one and only Son, so that everyone who believes in him will not perish but have eternal life.

Romans 10:9 . . . If you openly declare that Jesus is Lord and believe in your heart that God raised him from the dead, you will be saved.

Hebrews 2:14-15 . . . Because God's children are human beings—made of flesh and blood—the Son also became flesh and blood. For only as a human being could he die, and only by dying could he break the power of the devil, who had the power of death. Only in this way could he set free all who have lived their lives as slaves to the fear of dying.

Do not merely assume that you are a Christian and are going to Heaven. Make the conscious decision to repent of your sins and accept Christ's sacrificial death on your behalf. When you choose to place your faith in Christ and surrender control of your life to him, you can be certain that your name is written in the Lamb's Book of Life.

Romans 6:23 . . . The wages of sin is death, but the free gift of God is eternal life through Christ Jesus our Lord.

Titus 3:5 . . . He saved us, not because of the righteous things we had done, but because of his mercy. He washed away our sins, giving us a new birth and new life.

Ephesians 2:8-9 . . . God saved you by his grace when you believed. And you can't take credit for this; it is a gift from God. Salvation is not a reward for the good things we have done, so none of us can boast about it.

Sin has consequences, but God has provided a solution for our sin. Jesus Christ, the Son of God, loved us so much that he became a man to deliver us from our sin. He came to identify with us in our humanity and our weakness, but he did so without being tainted by our sin, self-deception, and moral failings. Even though we are under God's wrath for our sins, Jesus died on the cross as our representative, our substitute. Christ, who stood in our place, conveyed his righteousness to us so that we are declared innocent of all our sins and declared righteous and so that we may enter the presence of God in Heaven and be at home with him there.

God's Promises about Heaven

When you're wondering if there really is a Heaven . . .

Ecclesiastes 3:11 . . . God has made everything beautiful for its own time. He has planted eternity in the human heart, but even so, people cannot see the whole scope of God's work from beginning to end.

Revelation 21:3-4 . . . I heard a loud shout from the throne, saying, "Look, God's home is now among his people! He will live with them, and they will be his people. God himself will be with them. He will wipe every tear from their eyes, and there will be no more death or sorrow or crying or pain. All these things are gone forever."

When you're wondering what Heaven will be like . . .

2 Corinthians 5:1 . . . We know that when this earthly tent we live in is taken down (that is, when we die and leave this earthly body), we will have a house in heaven, an eternal body made for us by God himself and not by human hands.

Daniel 7:27 . . . The sovereignty, power, and greatness of all the kingdoms under heaven will be given to the holy people of the Most High.

Revelation 21:22-26 . . . I saw no temple in the city, for the Lord God Almighty and the Lamb are its temple. And the city has no need of sun or moon, for the glory of God illuminates the city, and the Lamb is its light. The nations will walk in its light, and the kings of the world will enter the city in all their glory. Its gates will never be closed at the end of day because there is no night there. And all the nations will bring their glory and honor into the city.

When you're wondering if there's a place for you in Heaven . . .

John 14:2 . . . There is more than enough room in my Father's home. If this were not so, would I have told you that I am going to prepare a place for you?

1 Peter 1:4-5 . . . We have a priceless inheritance— an inheritance that is kept in heaven for you, pure and undefiled, beyond the reach of change and decay. And through your faith, God is protecting you by his power until you receive this salvation, which is ready to be revealed on the last day for all to see.

When you're wondering if you will go to Heaven and how to get there . . .

Romans 10:9 . . . If you openly declare that Jesus is Lord and believe in your heart that God raised him from the dead, you will be saved.

John 6:47 . . . [Jesus said,] "I tell you the truth, anyone who believes has eternal life."

John 14:6 . . . Jesus [said], "I am the way, the truth, and the life. No one can come to the Father except through me."

Galatians 6:8 . . . Those who live only to satisfy their own sinful nature will harvest decay and death from that sinful nature. But those who live to please the Spirit will harvest everlasting life from the Spirit.

Hebrews 2:14-15 . . . Because God's children are human beings—made of flesh and blood—the Son also became flesh and blood. For only as a human being could he die, and only by dying could he break the power of the devil, who had the power of death. Only in this way could he set free all who have lived their lives as slaves to the fear of dying.

When you're afraid of dying . . .

> *John 11:25–26* . . . I am the resurrection and the life.
> Anyone who believes in me will live, even after dying.
> Everyone who lives in me and believes in me will
> never ever die.

> *Romans 6:23* . . . The wages of sin is death, but the
> free gift of God is eternal life through Christ Jesus
> our Lord.

> *1 Corinthians 15:43–44* . . . Our bodies are buried
> in brokenness, but they will be raised in glory. They
> are buried in weakness, but they will be raised in
> strength. They are buried as natural human bodies,
> but they will be raised as spiritual bodies.

When you doubt there is life after death . . .

Isaiah 26:19 . . . Those who die in the LORD will live; their bodies will rise again! Those who sleep in the earth will rise up and sing for joy! For your life-giving light will fall like dew on your people in the place of the dead!

John 3:16 . . . This is how God loved the world: He gave his one and only Son, so that everyone who believes in him will not perish but have eternal life.

Luke 23:43 . . . Jesus [said], "I assure you, today you will be with me in paradise."

When you're searching for happiness that lasts . . .

> *Psalm 16:11* . . . You will show me the way of life,
> granting me the joy of your presence and the
> pleasures of living with you forever.

> *1 Peter 5:4* . . . When the Great Shepherd appears,
> you will receive a crown of never-ending glory
> and honor.

When you long for something more than this world . . .

> *Hebrews 11:16* . . . They were looking for a better
> place, a heavenly homeland. That is why God is not
> ashamed to be called their God, for he has prepared
> a city for them.

> *Hebrews 13:14* . . . This world is not our permanent
> home; we are looking forward to a home yet to come.

Scripture Index

Genesis 1:24-25 . . . *101*
Genesis 1:26-28 . . . *79*
Genesis 1:27 . . . *139*
Genesis 2:2 . . . *207*
Genesis 2:7 . . . *14, 206*
Genesis 2:8-9 . . . *168, 235*
Genesis 2:15 . . . *242*
Genesis 2:15-17 . . . *112*
Genesis 2:18 . . . *192*
Genesis 2:18-19 . . . *94*
Genesis 3:1 . . . *96*
Genesis 3:22-23 . . . *235*
Genesis 3:4-7, 17, 23 . . . *112*
Genesis 11:1, 4-7 . . . *159*

Exodus 15:20 . . . *126*
Exodus 20:9-11 . . . *207*
Exodus 25:10-11 . . . *249*
Exodus 26:1 . . . *249*
Exodus 31:1-5 . . . *248*
Exodus 33:18-23 . . . *64*

Leviticus 25:4-5 . . . *207*
Leviticus 26:6 . . . *216*
Leviticus 26:11-12 . . . *68*

Deuteronomy 29:29 . . . *45*

Joshua 24:15 . . . *51*

2 Samuel 6:16 . . . *126*

1 Chronicles 25:6 . . . *165*

2 Kings 2:11-12 . . . *17*

Job 19:25-27 . . . *62, 65*
Job 19:26 . . . *206*
Job 19:26-27 . . . *148*
Job 37:3-6 . . . *240*

Psalm 4:8 . . . *216*
Psalm 8:6-8 . . . *94*
Psalm 16:11 . . . *114, 266*
Psalm 19:1 . . . *221*
Psalm 37:4 . . . *121*

Psalm 56:8 ... *109*

Psalm 72:8, 11 ... *75*

Psalm 103:11 ... *212*

Psalm 104:33 ... *165*

Psalm 119:18 ... *43*

Psalm 119:89 ... *109*

Psalm 139:14 ... *108*

Psalm 148:3-6 ... *219*

Psalm 148:7, 10-13 ... *99*

Psalm 150:3-6 ... *165*

Proverbs 12:10 ... *94*

Proverbs 22:2 ... *128*

Ecclesiastes 3:11 ... *259*

Ecclesiastes 12:7 ... *7*

Isaiah 6:1-2 ... *46*

Isaiah 11:6-8 ... *92*

Isaiah 11:6-9 ... *86*

Isaiah 14:12-15 ... *41*

Isaiah 25:6 ... *71, 134*

Isaiah 26:19 ... *265*

Isaiah 35:1 ... *171*

Isaiah 51:3 ... *171*

Isaiah 55:13 ... *169*

Isaiah 59:2 ... *50*

Isaiah 60:19-21 ... *223*

Isaiah 65:16 ... *199*

Isaiah 65:17 ... *37, 88, 188, 218, 221*

Isaiah 65:17, 21 ... *143*

Isaiah 65:17, 25 ... *92*

Isaiah 66:22 ... *146*

Jeremiah 31:34 ... *199*

Ezekiel 1:1 ... *47*

Ezekiel 34:25-26 ... *216*

Ezekiel 34:26-27 ... *241*

Ezekiel 36:35 ... *169*

Ezekiel 37:27 ... *68*

Daniel 7:27 ... *78, 119, 260*

Daniel 9:23 ... *233*

Daniel 10:13 ... *90*

Daniel 12:13 ... *186*

Hosea 2:16, 19-20 ... *212*

Amos 9:13-14 ... *242*

Malachi 3:16-18 ... *110*

Matthew 6:19-20 ... *210*

Matthew 6:19-21 ... *26*

Matthew 6:20 ... *186*

Matthew 7:13 ... *141*

Matthew 7:13-14 ... *50*

Matthew 8:11 ... *133, 137, 149*

Matthew 10:28 ... *54*

Matthew 12:36 ... *26*

Matthew 13:40-42 ... *54*

Matthew 13:41 ... *214*

Matthew 19:28 ... *157*

Matthew 20:28 . . . *71*
Matthew 22:30 . . . *163, 212*
Matthew 22:37-39 . . . *193*
Matthew 24:35 . . . *109*
Matthew 25:23 . . . *77, 243*
Matthew 25:46 . . . *54*
Matthew 26:29 . . . *146*

Mark 10:14-15 . . . *125*
Mark 10:29-30 . . . *130*
Mark 13:27 . . . *185*

Luke 2:52 . . . *154*
Luke 6:20-23 . . . *238*
Luke 6:21 . . . *103, 124, 161*
Luke 6:21-23 . . . *197*
Luke 6:23 . . . *161*
Luke 8:21 . . . *130*
Luke 9:30-31 . . . *29*
Luke 12:37 . . . *72*
Luke 14:14 . . . *210*
Luke 15:7 . . . *149*
Luke 15:10 . . . *30, 103*
Luke 15:25-27 . . . *126*
Luke 16:9 . . . *143, 190*
Luke 16:10 . . . *77*
Luke 16:12 . . . *186*
Luke 16:22-24 . . . *7*
Luke 16:24-25 . . . *33, 200*
Luke 16:25 . . . *25, 147*
Luke 19:17-19 . . . *245*

Luke 21:33 . . . *58*
Luke 22:18 . . . *133*
Luke 22:29-30 . . . *133*
Luke 23:43 . . . *7, 265*
Luke 24:31 . . . *83*
Luke 24:39 . . . *145, 147, 185*

John 3:16 . . . *253, 265*
John 4:34 . . . *244*
John 5:17 . . . *244*
John 5:28-29 . . . *52*
John 6:47 . . . *262*
John 8:44 . . . *41*
John 11:25-26 . . . *264*
John 13:8 . . . *71*
John 14:2 . . . *48, 143, 190, 261*
John 14:2-3 . . . *168*
John 14:3 . . . *48*
John 14:6 . . . *262*
John 20:14-16 . . . *139*
John 20:16 . . . *145*
John 20:19 . . . *83*
John 20:27 . . . *195, 200*
John 20:27-28 . . . *145*
John 21:12 . . . *195*
John 21:12-14 . . . *132*
John 21:12-15 . . . *145*

Acts 1:9 . . . *83*
Acts 1:11 . . . *16*
Acts 3:21 . . . *59*

Acts 9:4-5 ... *34*
Acts 10:34-35 ... *128*
Acts 17:26 ... *137*

Romans 1:19-20 ... *141*
Romans 1:20 ... *66*
Romans 3:23 ... *50*
Romans 5:18-19 ... *135*
Romans 6:7 ... *215*
Romans 6:23 ... *214,*
    254, 264
Romans 8:18 ... *239*
Romans 8:18-23 ... *183*
Romans 8:19-23 ... *58*
Romans 10:9 ... *253, 262*
Romans 11:29 ... *229*
Romans 14:10-12 ... *20*

1 Corinthians 2:9-10 ... *45*
1 Corinthians 3:13-14 ... *20, 59*
1 Corinthians 6:2-3 ... *75, 90*
1 Corinthians 9:24 ... *225*
1 Corinthians 12:14-17 ... *128*
1 Corinthians 13:12 ... *62, 152*
1 Corinthians 15:6 ... *195*
1 Corinthians 15:17-19 ... *204*
1 Corinthians 15:26 ... *232*
1 Corinthians 15:42 ... *253*
1 Corinthians 15:43-44 ... *264*
1 Corinthians 15:49 ... *204*
1 Corinthians 15:53 ... *84*

2 Corinthians 3:18 ... *66, 155*
2 Corinthians 5:1 ... *260*
2 Corinthians 5:3 ... *107*
2 Corinthians 5:8 ... *7, 91*
2 Corinthians 5:10 ... *20,*
    25, 186
2 Corinthians 5:17 ... *60, 157*
2 Corinthians 6:16 ... *68*
2 Corinthians 12:3 ... *16*

Galatians 6:8 ... *262*

Ephesians 1:10 ... *56*
Ephesians 2:6-7 ... *117, 154*
Ephesians 2:7 ... *233*
Ephesians 2:8-9 ... *19, 255*
Ephesians 2:10 ... *245*
Ephesians 5:31-32 ... *163*

Philippians 1:23 ... *3*
Philippians 3:20-21 ... *107, 204*
Philippians 3:21 ... *83, 132*

Colossians 3:23 ... *243*
Colossians 3:23-24 ... *250*
Colossians 3:24 ... *186*

1 Thessalonians 2:17 ... *192*
1 Thessalonians 2:19-20 ... *193*
1 Thessalonians 4:13 ... *3*
1 Thessalonians 4:13-18 ... *195*

2 Timothy 2:5 ... *225*
2 Timothy 2:7 ... *43*

Titus 3:5 ... *19, 254*

Hebrews 1:14 ... *90*
Hebrews 2:14-15 ... *254, 262*
Hebrews 4:3 ... *208*
Hebrews 4:9 ... *208*
Hebrews 8:5 ... *10*
Hebrews 8:10 ... *121*
Hebrews 10:10 ... *214*
Hebrews 11:5 ... *17*
Hebrews 11:10 ... *179*
Hebrews 11:16 ... *69, 267*
Hebrews 12:14 ... *65*
Hebrews 12:22 ... *12, 176*
Hebrews 12:28 ... *174*
Hebrews 13:14 ... *267*

James 4:14 ... *51*

1 Peter 1:3-4 ... *188*
1 Peter 1:4-5 ... *261*
1 Peter 1:12 ... *152*
1 Peter 5:4 ... *266*

2 Peter 3:10 ... *58*
2 Peter 3:13 ... *197, 221*

1 John 2:2 ... *141*
1 John 5:13 ... *253*

Revelation 1:1-2 ... *46*
Revelation 2:7 ... *12, 133, 235*
Revelation 2:10 ... *76*

Revelation 2:17 ... *187, 190*
Revelation 2:28 ... *219*
Revelation 3:11 ... *76*
Revelation 3:15 ... *30*
Revelation 4:8-9 ... *100*
Revelation 4:10 ... *76, 231*
Revelation 5:1 ... *110*
Revelation 5:9 ... *105*
Revelation 5:9-10 ... *150*
Revelation 5:13 ... *73, 97, 99*
Revelation 5:14 ... *73*
Revelation 6:9-10 ... *8, 24, 28, 199*
Revelation 6:9-11 ... *22*
Revelation 6:10 ... *32, 123*
Revelation 6:10-11 ... *230*
Revelation 6:11 ... *115*
Revelation 7:9 ... *10, 105, 115*
Revelation 7:9, 12 ... *74*
Revelation 7:10 ... *159*
Revelation 7:11 ... *73, 123*
Revelation 8:1 ... *231*
Revelation 8:6 ... *10*
Revelation 8:7, 13 ... *166*
Revelation 8:13 ... *10, 97*
Revelation 10:2 ... *110*
Revelation 10:9-10 ... *15*
Revelation 12:7 ... *90*
Revelation 12:10-12 ... *33*
Revelation 13:5-6 ... *112*

Revelation 13:6 ... *41*

Revelation 14:3 ... *166*

Revelation 14:13 ... *26, 208, 247*

Revelation 15:2-3 ... *166*

Revelation 15:6 ... *116*

Revelation 18:20 ... *28*

Revelation 19:1-2 ... *29*

Revelation 20:12 ... *109*

Revelation 20:15 ... *52*

Revelation 21:1 ... *5, 58, 63, 180*

Revelation 21:1-3 ... *218*

Revelation 21:2 ... *176, 235*

Revelation 21:2-4 ... *37*

Revelation 21:2, 10-11, 18, 21 ... *227*

Revelation 21:3 ... *56*

Revelation 21:3-4 ... *259*

Revelation 21:4 ... *35, 123, 214*

Revelation 21:5 ... *101, 154*

Revelation 21:10 ... *173*

Revelation 21:10-11 ... *48*

Revelation 21:10-12 ... *178*

Revelation 21:12 ... *201*

Revelation 21:14 ... *201*

Revelation 21:15-16 ... *48*

Revelation 21:15-16, 19 ... *176*

Revelation 21:21 ... *178*

Revelation 21:22 ... *69*

Revelation 21:22-26 ... *260*

Revelation 21:23 ... *223*

Revelation 21:26 ... *119*

Revelation 21:27 ... *51*

Revelation 22:1-2 ... *181, 203*

Revelation 22:2 ... *230, 237*

Revelation 22:3 ... *242*

Revelation 22:3-4 ... *64*

Revelation 22:5 ... *75, 175, 223*

Revelation 22:14 ... *69*

About the Author

RANDY ALCORN is the founder and director of Eternal Perspective Ministries and a *New York Times* bestselling author of more than forty books including *Heaven* (over one million sold), *If God Is Good, The Treasure Principle,* and the Gold Medallion winner *Safely Home.* His books in print exceed seven million and have been translated into more than fifty languages.

Alcorn resides in Gresham, Oregon, with his wife, Nanci. They have two married daughters and five grandsons. Randy enjoys hanging out with his family, biking, tennis, research, and reading.

You may contact Eternal Perspective Ministries online at www.epm.org; by mail at 39085 Pioneer Blvd., Suite 206, Sandy, OR 97055; or by phone at 503.668.5200. Follow Randy on Facebook: www.facebook.com/randyalcorn, Twitter: www.twitter.com/randyalcorn, and on his blog: www.epm.org/blog.

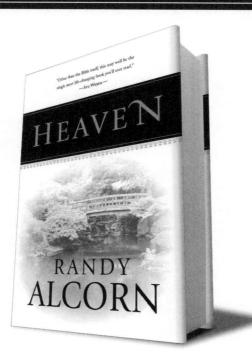